Elizabeth Rex

Other plays by Timothy Findley
available from Blizzard Publishing

The Stillborn Lover
The Trials of Ezra Pound

Elizabeth Rex

by Timothy Findley

BLIZZARD PUBLISHING
Winnipeg • Niagara Falls

First published 2000 in Canada and the United States by
Blizzard Publishing Inc.
73 Furby Street, Winnipeg, Canada R3C 2A2.

Distributed in the United States by General Distribution Services,
4500 Witmer Industrial Estates, Niagara Falls, NY 14305–1386.

Cover art by Michael Rafelson.
Cover design by Otium.
Printed for Blizzard Publishing in Canada by Kromar.

5   4   3   2   1

Blizzard Publishing gratefully acknowledges the support of
Canadian Heritage, the Manitoba Arts Council, and the
Canada Council for the Arts to its publishing program.

Cataloguing in Publication Data

Findley, Timothy, 1930–
   Elizabeth Rex
   A play.
   ISBN 0-921368-98-4
1. Elizabeth I, Queen of England, 1533–1603—Drama.
2. Shakespeare, William, 1564–1616—Drama. I. Title.
PS8511.I38E45 2000   C812'.54   C00-920128-9
PR9199.3.F52E45 2000

For Martha Henry, Brent Carver,
Diane D'Aquila, and Peter Hutt

Come,
Let's have one other gaudy night: call to me
All my sad captains; fill our bowls once more:
Let's mock the midnight bell.

—William Shakespeare
Antony and Cleopatra, *III, xiii*

Elizabeth Rex was first produced by the Stratford Festival and premièred at the Tom Patterson Theatre in Stratford, Ontario on June 29, 2000 with the following cast:

ELIZABETH	Diane D'Aquila
NED	Brent Carver
WILL	Peter Hutt
JACK	Scott Wentworth
CECIL	Bernard Hopkins
TARDY	Joyce Campion
PERCY	Keith Dinicol
HARRY	Paul Dunn
STANLEY	Florence MacGregor
HENSLOWE	Rita Howell
BEAR	Aaron Franks
LUDDY	Michael Fawkes
MATT	Evan Buliung
TOM	Damien Atkins
BEN	Andrew Burr
Servants	Wayne Davis, Pragna Desai, Andy Pogson, and Rose Ryan

Directed by Martha Henry
Sets and costumes by Allan Wilbee
Lighting designed by Louise Guinand
Original music by Stephen Woodjetts
Sound designed by Todd Charlton
Choreography and movement by John Broome
Fights directed by James Binkley
Assistant Director: Andrew Freund
Stage Manager: Lauren Snell
Assistant Stage Managers: Renate Hanson, Milissa Rood,
Helen Himsl, Michael Hart
Design Assistant: Bonnie Deakin
Lighting Design Assistant: Andrew McCaw

Playwright's Note

I would first like to acknowledge the contribution of Paul Thompson to the development of this play. Paul not only directed the Stratford Festival's workshop of an early draft, but also— through all the subsequent drafts—directed private workshops in which the only participant was the playwright, who was asked to perform each of the major characters. It was in these "bear-pit" sessions that a better understanding emerged as to who these people were, and how they interacted.

This play was born in answer to a conundrum that has fascinated me for years: because women were not allowed to appear on stage in Elizabethan theatre, the female roles were played by so-called "boy actors"—but who played the women of a maturity and depth far beyond the range of any boy? Who played Cleopatra—Lady Macbeth—Mad Margaret? It seemed to me that there must have been actors in Shakespeare's time who had passed well beyond boyhood, and who therefore could undertake such strong and demanding female roles. Without such men, would Shakespeare have written such women? And so I invented a mature leading actor of female roles—Ned Lowenscroft.

Pondering the whole question of a contradiction of genders, I remembered that Elizabeth I often referred to herself as "a Prince of Europe" and even declared that in order to maintain her grasp on the British monarchy and to rule her England, she was called upon to be more man than woman. Suddenly, a phrase drifted into my mind. *Elizabeth Rex,* "King Elizabeth."

Here, then, was the possibility of a glorious, theatrical confrontation—between the woman who throughout her reign had played the role of a man, and the man who in his theatrical career had played the role of a woman. To make the most of the confrontation, I decided it must take place at some moment when the monarch felt it necessary to recapture her womanhood, just as the actor finally required—for whatever reason—the full strength of his manhood.

History provided such a moment. Two years before her death, the Queen's lover, Robert Devereux, the Earl of Essex, raised a rebellion against her. If Elizabeth, the monarch, had to condemn him to death, where did this leave Elizabeth, the woman? Fiction was then able to step in and give the actor a disease that in those days was often fatal—syphilis. Was he man enough to face his own imminent death?

History offered further help. Essex, imprisoned in the Tower of London, was to be beheaded in the early morning hours of Ash Wednesday, 1601. On the eve of his execution, Shrove Tuesday, it is known that Elizabeth called Shakespeare and his actors—the Lord Chamberlain's Men—to perform in one of her palaces. She sought distraction from the torment of what her royal duty had forced her to do. It is not recorded which play was presented on that occasion, and so I was free to have it be *Much Ado About Nothing*. To me, Elizabeth would have loved the character of Beatrice, one of the strongest and most independent women in the Shakespeare canon. This way, I was also able to have the Queen become intrigued by the actor who brought this woman to life.

History provided one more fascinating twist. The nobleman who was imprisoned with Essex for taking part in the rebellion was Harry Wriothesley, Earl of Southampton—the playwright's wealthy patron and, according to some, the true love of Shakespeare's life. (By the way, if Harry's name baffles you, it can be pronounced either of two ways: *Risely* or *Rosely*. We have chosen *Rosely* for the play.)

Shakespeare, who was actually writing *Hamlet* in this period, is shown to be in the early stages of creating *Antony and Cleopatra*— a play that was not performed until after the death of Elizabeth. Many scholars believe this was because it told a story too close for comfort to that of Elizabeth and Essex.

What emerged, for me, from this barn filled with contradictions and emotional conflicts, was a sense that neither gender nor sexuality, politics nor ambition, are as important as integrity. As Shrove Tuesday passes into Ash Wednesday, playwright, player, and Queen must come to terms with who they truly are, and how they will cope with the inevitable. This echoes Polonius's advice in *Hamlet:* "This above all, to thine own self be true." Or, as Glenn Gould was to declare to me a year before his death: "all that matters is that you become yourself."

Timothy Findley
Stratford, Ontario
June 2000

Characters

The names in brackets are the characters played in *Much Ado About Nothing*, just before the main action of the play begins.

The Lord Chamberlain's Men (in order of appearance):

WILL: William Shakespeare, actor-playwright and shareholder of The Lord Chamberlain's Men; fifty-two.

NED: Edward Lowenscroft, actor; mid-thirties. (Beatrice)

JACK: Jonathan Edmund, actor; late thirties. (Benedick)

MATT: Matthew Welles, actor; twenties. (Claudio)

PERCY: Percy Gower, character actor; sixties. (Watch)

HARRY: Henry Pearle, actor; eighteen. (Hero)

TOM: Tom Travis, boy actor; late teens. (Margaret)

BEN: Benjamin Herlie, boy actor; late teens. (Boy)

TARDY: Kate Tardwell, the wardrobe mistress or "'tire woman"; fifties.

LUDDY: Luddy Beddoes, character actor; fifties. (Friar Francis)

BEAR: Ned Lowenscroft's tame bear.

The Court (in order of appearance):

STANLEY: Lady Mary Stanley, early twenties; maid of honour to the Queen.

ELIZABETH: Queen Elizabeth I; sixty-seven.

HENSLOWE: Anne, Countess of Henslowe, lady-in-waiting to the Queen; seventies.

CECIL: Lord Robert Cecil, Private Secretary to the Queen; thirty-eight.

Servants, Watch, etc.

11

The Set

The play takes place in the whitewashed interior of a barn in Stratford-upon-Avon on the night of April 22, 1616 until dawn the following morning. At the rear, a barnyard is visible beyond tall wooden doors that stand open. There is an exit upstage right into the further reaches of the barn. There are hay lofts above either side of the upstage area, each reached by its own ladder. The upstage area is raised, with two broad steps leading down. Slightly off centre, a brazier waits to be lighted. A basket of fuel sits nearby. Various theatrical accoutrements are also seen: some wicker skips containing properties and costumes which spill over their sides; a cluster of box-trees and a rosebush; a box of books; a bundle of furled standards; a keg of ale on a tripod; a barrel of water, plus a bucket; a prince's chair, a bench and some wooden stools. There is straw on parts of the floor. Above the lofts, a banner is loosely hung, which reads: "The Lord Chamberlain's Men." On the night of Shakespeare's death, it is in this setting—filled with relics of his London days—that the playwright conjures another barn and another night—Shrove Tuesday, 1601.

Prologue

(The barn, Stratford-upon-Avon; night, April 22, 1616. The interior is lit with ghostly light.)

NED: *(Off, singing a cappella.)*
Fear no more the heat o' the sun,
Nor the furious winter's rages;
Thou thy worldly task hast done,
Home art gone and ta'en thy wages;
Golden lads and girls all must,
As chimney-sweepers, come to dust.

(A bell tolls.

A light appears in the barnyard.

WILL enters, carrying a lantern. He wears a long robe of the sort worn before retiring. Under this, he wears a loose shirt and hastily drawn on Jacobean trousers and hose. He is slippered. There is a scarf about his neck and woollen gloves on his hands. He is fifty-two years old.)

WILL: There you are, then—somebody's Passing-bell ... *(Lighting a taper from his lantern, he lights the brazier.)* Tomorrow, it will ring for me. "Young Will Shakespeare died this day ..." That's what they'll tell you. "Died this day that was his birthday. Fifty-two years old ... Lay back and died. In his bed. Like a child." Trouble is—I'm not in my bed and I won't lie down. I'd rather be out here, in my barn.

(He looks about him, spies a box of books and begins to rummage as he speaks. He puts a small book, a notebook, and a pencil in his pocket.)

My whole life is out here—*(He flips the pages of a book.)*—the whole of my life ... I'd come here naked, as a boy—straight from that river out there—throw my clothes on the floor and climb up into that loft and lie there dreaming in the hay ...

BOYS: *(Off, calling.)* Will! Will! Where are you? Hurry up ...

13

(Sound: water, birds, insects.)

WILL: All those summer days—scouring the banks of the Avon for smooth, round stones—scaring up ducks and foxes—kingfishers—swallows ...

(Distant dog barking.)

... somebody's dog ... Oh, God—I want it back. Throwing stones that never reached the other shore.

(He throws a book back into the box.

Sound: a stone plunges into water.)

And the games—the games—the games, and all my friends ...

BOYS: *(Off.)* Will! Will! Over here! Over here!

WILL: ... the river making off with our lives—all of us swept downstream and God knows where we'd land ... Well—I landed here. Right where I began. This barn is the only theatre I have left. This—and the one in here. *(His mind.)* And these. *(The book box.)* Mere echoes of what there was. Cold now—for April. Not the Aprils I remember. So be it. That's what they'll say I died of—*a chill.* Went out a week ago—having spent the day, the evening, the night with my friend Ben Jonson. Two drunken playwrights—both of us overfed and over-aled. Stood in the rain, and the cold and the wind, and the wind blew all the way through me ...

(Sound: a dog barks.)

Who am I talking to? *Who goes there? Give me a moment! Let me have one—last—moment!!*

(A ghost BEAR appears from the gutters and heads upstage centre towards the barnyard. As it passes WILL, he reaches one hand toward the figure, but the BEAR continues on and exits.)

I know who you are! I know what's happening here! I know what's happening! Leave me alone! I could not—I *cannot* write you! Oh—dearest Jesu—why, in this final moment, *this?* This, that I could not and *cannot* achieve ... the telling of that moment. The telling of that night.

(He pulls a stone jar from his pocket and drinks. Then he goes to one of the skips and pulls out articles of costume.)

What should a person wear to die in? I have been so many ... lived so many other lives. And all the while, my own life burning down around me while I barely noticed it—failed to live it. And now, it's over. Nearly. Not quite. Almost. And that unwritten night ... These were the flags they wore—the emblems of who they were: *the tunic of a soldier ... the bodice of a Queen ... the bells of a clown ... the gown of a Beatrice ...* purchased, I might add, at some expense—*and the cap of a scholar ...*

(Having laid the others aside, he regards the scholar's cap.)

I put this on my head each time I wrote. It was my only ritual.

(He puts it on as if it were the crown.)

"Down it will come—and words will follow. Flow." Or so I prayed.

(He takes off the cap.)

These are the only truths I know—I know no other truths but these. We play so many roles before we die—and then ... we die.

(The bell tolls nine.)

I'm not ready. Not yet ... Don't!

(The dog barks.)

Barking dogs ... Shrove Tuesday. Ash Wednesday. 1601. The beginning of the ending of my world.

(He puts on the scholar's cap, turns to the barn doors and quotes.)

"You are welcome, masters. Welcome, all."

(From the courtyard, four of the players drag on a cart with props and a skip on board. The actors are costumed for Much Ado About Nothing. *PERCY GOWER jangles bells. JACK EDMUND carries a tattered banner. MATT WELLES is the drummer. JACK and MATT wear scarlet tunics. The fourth player is a woman. They cross the stage. The woman moves to the brazier. She pulls off her wig and throws it down.)*

NED: Shit!

(Clearly, a man has spoken.

The lights alter. We are in the past.)

Act One
Shrove Tuesday, 1601

Scene One

(NED LOWENSCROFT is in his thirties. Strands and tufts of hair hang down, and there are open sores on his head. He wears white make-up, with rouged cheeks and lips. His gown is black, the bodice already standing open.)

NED: Shit! Shit! Shit!

(He tries to undo more of his costume.)

WILL: You'll wear yourself out with shitting, if you're not careful.

NED: I'll shit when I please.

WILL: Mind what you do to that costume, Ned. It cost me a good deal of money.

NED: Piss on your money. If you spent more, you could afford a half-decent actor.

WILL: I assume you aren't referring to yourself.

NED: Damn right I'm not. I'm referring to that bitch, Edmund.

(He removes a shoe and throws it at JACK.)

WILL: Jack? Next to you and Dick Burbage, Ned, he's the best we have.

NED: Best what? Arse-licker?

WILL: Now, now ...

NED: Tell him to learn his lines!

WILL: Learn your lines, Master Edmund. *(To NED.)* Which lines?

NED: Ask *him*. The bitch.

(He throws a second shoe.)

WILL: Why? How can Master Edmund name what he forgot?

JACK: *(Picking up the shoes.)* I forgot to say: "Tarry, sweet Beatrice ..."

NED: Yes! And a lot of good that does me now! Out there—I near walked off the stage because you didn't call me back.

16

JACK: It was only one line.

(He throws the shoes at the skip.)

WILL: Here! Mind those shoes!

NED: *Not* only one line! It was my cue to turn! I near fell off the edge. I near fell off the god-damned edge. I near fell off the god-damned rutting edge! The god-damned rutting edge, you god-damned rutting whore!

WILL: I think we get your point, Ned.

NED: No. You do not! *(He shouts in JACK's face.)* Near fell off the god-damned rutting edge!! In front of the god-damned rutting Queen!! You god-damned rutting bitch!!

JACK: You've been drinking again, haven't you.

(NED kisses him. JACK recoils in genuine horror.)

Dear Christ in heaven! Don't! *(He wipes his mouth.)* Not on my lips, you bastard! Not on my lips, you diseased bastard ... Oh, Christ ...

(He crosses to the bucket and throws water on his face.)

WILL: The disease is not in his lips, Jack. His spittle will not harm you. "Tarry, sweet Beatrice ..."

NED: Oh, God—what have I done ...

WILL: Nothing. No harm. None. Say your next line.

NED: Oh ...

WILL: Come along, now. "Tarry, sweet Beatrice ..."

NED: "I am gone, though I am here; there is no love in you; nay— I pray you, let me go."

WILL: "Beatrice ..."

NED: "In faith, I will go."

(NED steps from the gown.)

WILL: *(Whispering.)* Benedick ...

JACK: "We'll be friends first ..."

NED: "You dare easier be friends with me than fight with mine enemy."

JACK: "Is Claudio thine enemy?"

NED: "Is 'a not approved in the height a villain ..." *(He now attempts to remove his underskirt.)* "... that hath slandered, scorned, dishonoured my kinswoman?" *(He tears the underskirt away.)* "O, that I were a man!"

(NED wears tights, a shirt, and a bourrelet, which gives him the outlines of female hips.)

JACK: There. Are you satisfied ... my man?

NED: Maybe. Maybe not. I should not have kissed you.

JACK: True.

(WILL picks up the discarded underskirt, sees it is ripped, and throws up his arms in despair.)

NED: I should have "eaten your heart in the market place," you bugger! And me, near falling off the edge into the Queen's lap ...

JACK: If you had, she would have loved you for it.

NED: I dare say. If I were not diseased ... I should not have done that. Jack. I'm sorry.

JACK: It's gone, now. Washed away.

(NED takes the underskirt from WILL and crosses to the skips, where he deposits skirt and bourrelet, removes a stone jar of liquor from its hiding place, and drinks.)

PERCY: "I near fell off the edge! I near fell off the god-damned edge! I near fell off the god-damned rutting edge! The god-damned rutting edge, you god-damned rutting whore!" I wish I had that much to say.

WILL: Stop complaining—

PERCY: I have a right to complain. I'm old—and you never give me nothing to speak no more.

WILL: If you could keep a sentence straight, Percy, I might.

PERCY: Nothing to say. Not one word. Nor dancing. Nor the songs I once sang—in my youth ...

MATT: We don't want to hear about your youth, old man.

PERCY: In my youth ... *in my youth,* I played a prettier girl than any boy you ever saw. In my youth, I had a pair of legs that killed, in britches parts. Killed men dead! *Dead*—they did. I had a leg you'd hardly know was human. Men sent me flowers. Flowers in parcels. Parcels of them! Par-cels. In my youth ...

WILL: In your youth I hope you had the sense to keep your mouth shut. You're tiresome as a wife.

PERCY: I put a lot of money in your pocket, Will Shakespeare. In my time—much money. You got no right to speak to me that way. I put a packet in your pocket. Me as Jacques. Me as Feste. Me as Shallow. "Jesu! Jesu! The mad days that I have spent ..." You wrote that out for me, Will. And now, you give me nought to speak—*nought*—I that was your prince of clowns.

(Three more players enter, carrying lanterns. TOM and HARRY— boys as women—and BEN as a boy. BEN carries a basket.)

JACK: Any news? Surely we aren't stuck here for the night?

HARRY: Yes … All the others got away before the last bell. We're the only actors left.

BEN: There's a curfew. They've locked the gates!

HARRY: It's still not safe in the streets. Won't be, till the cannons fire in the morning. That's what they said.

MATT: Really?

(HARRY nods.)

Dammit—so we're still prisoners.

JACK: And—*voila!*—no London, no divine Olivia …

MATT: We'll never see *her* again.

JACK: Maybe you won't—but I will.

TOM: I'm not one bit sorry we're here. I've never been in a palace before.

BEN: I've never been out of London before. *(He hands the basket to MATT.)* Here's food we stole for them as didn't eat.

MATT: You're very good at that, young Ben. More than a useful talent for a starving actor.

BEN: We was fed in the kitchen! I had the whole of one chicken, all to myself. Tom wasn't hungry, was you, Tom.

TOM: No. They gave me wine and it made me sick.

PERCY: Tempting young boys. That's the way it was with me. Plies you with drink—then it's down with the britches and into the dark. You mind, Tom. I told you a thousand times.

HARRY: I was there. Nothing happened. I wouldn't let it.

PERCY: Men and women—each has dangers. You mark my words.

(TOM removes his female clothing and throws it onto the floor. He still wears his female wig and make-up. HARRY removes only his wig.)

NED: Oh, for God's sake! It didn't happen. Talk about something else!

PERCY: I could give you "all the world's a stage …"

ALL: *(Speaking in tired unison.)* "… and all the men and women merely players …" *(Some make rude noises.)*

PERCY: It was only a suggestion.

MATT: Sit on it.

(PERCY sits, and as he sits, he "farts.")

PERCY: I can still play a fart on cue. I'm not a dead loss, you know.

(From the courtyard, there is distant laughter and applause. Spirited music is heard—with pipes and drums. TOM makes an attempt at a solo courtly dance.)

BEN: Come along, Tom—this is the way they do it! You be my Lady and I'll be your Lord ...

(They dance near PERCY, who joins in. WILL sits on the steps, takes the small book from his pocket and reads.)

Scene Two

TARDY: *(Off.)* Here! You lads!

(Kate Tardwell, known as TARDY, appears in the barnyard. She is slightly tiddly, and attempting to balance at least three hats on her head, while her arms are loaded down with skirts, jerkins, ruffs, sword belts, etc. She moves as if avoiding obstacles.)

TARDY: Is nobody there? Help poor Tardy. It's me, fellows! Kate! Get busy, or I'll drop the whole lot in the yard manure—an' you'll wear 'em, stink or not! Seven hats, and four need mending— three white shifts, and two is torn. Them that ran to the city, 'fore the curfew was set. Look—they ripped half my stitches in their hurry. And none of you is better, stay or go!

(BEN, TOM, and HARRY go to her and lift off parts of her bundles. The hats stay on her head; her spectacles sit on the uppermost hat, their arms around its crown.)

Wantons! Stripping off these pretty pieces—throwing them in all directions! And only me to find them. Now, my spectacles is lost. Gone. And all this work to do before morning ... You seen 'em? My specs?

(TOM removes the spectacles from the hat and puts them on.)

TOM: No, Tardy.

(HARRY grabs the spectacles from TOM and puts them on.)

TARDY: You?

HARRY: On your nose, last time I saw them.

(BEN steals them from HARRY and puts them on.)

TARDY: You?

BEN: Never.

TARDY: I know that voice. Don't give me *never*, Master Rascal! It's you took 'em off me twice before.

BEN: Never, Tardy. Swear.

(TOM grabs the spectacles from BEN and puts them on TARDY's own cap, so they rest above her forehead.)

TARDY: Well, one of you did. Someone did. I'll take my ale, now, thank you. If I can find my way.

(She heads for the keg, bumping into MATT as she goes.)

Who's that? You, is it, Master Matthew. Get me some ale, same as always—there's a good fellow.

MATT: Right away, Kate.

(He goes to the keg and fills a tankard.)

TARDY: *(Putting her hand out.)* There's fines for rending 'tires—and I want them now. Morning will come and London with it and I'll want more threads ...

(She goes about collecting pennies from the actors.)

Pay up, clumsy louts and ruffians ... Here! That was tuppence from you! None of that making off with my profits. I got expenses same as you and a husband's grave to tend, besides. Tore it straight through, you did, that doublet I mended only yesterday. *(She puts the collected money in a cloth purse.)* I never been in a Queen's barn before. It don't half smell horsy.

(Music. Cries of approval, applause—from off.)

All them lords and ladies, dancing delighted, but the Queen does her dancing from a broken heart. Makes a person wonder what her Council's up to, don't it—what with Essex on the block. Proper bastard, that's what he is, that Essex. As for that other— the Earl of Southampton—the one she Towered with him—he's as much a proper bastard as his friend. The two of them— treasoners!

MATT: *(Handing her ale.)* There you go.

TARDY: Bliss on earth ...

JACK: Don't tell me *you* were in love with Essex, too.

TARDY: I think not. He never pays his debts, either—same as you lot.

(JACK and MATT laugh.)

Oh, yes! A manly laugh. A woman gets used to man's laughter— the scorn of it—the leer of it. And the rage.

JACK: The rage, Kate?

TARDY: Aye. That a woman has more 'pacity for love than a man. So a fellow has to mock it—make it seem Cheapside, for fear we find him standing in the shallows when it comes to his own 'pacity for love.

MATT: 'Pacity, Kate?

TARDY: 'Pacity. Yes. Some such word. I heard it only once, but I know what it means.

NED: "She had a sweet capacity for love."

TARDY: That's it. A sweet capacity. *She* had, mark you.

NED: "And he had none."

TARDY: "And he had none." You spoke it, Master Ned. I don't remember where.

NED: *Love's Labour's Lost.*

TARDY: "A sweet capacity for love ..." A well-writ phrase.

WILL: We cut it.

(She tries to set the empty tankard in place. It falls.)

TARDY: See that? Without my specs, I'm blind as a belfry. And my eyes required for six more hours of stitching. If I discover one of you lads scuppered with them, there'll be more than one beheading in the morning.

(She starts off, up left.)

JACK: You leaving us without the benefit of female company, Kate? We want your 'pacity ...

TARDY: Hah! You'll never lack for female company, Master Edmund. Not till you hit the grave. And even there, I'd have me doubts.

(TARDY exits into the deeper reaches of the barn up left.)

MATT: That's our Tardy—poor old woman.

NED: Best be careful. Next you know, she'll use your cod-piece for a pin cushion.

(He sits close to WILL, who is still reading the book.)

WILL: Must you sit there?

NED: Yes. Do you always move your lips when you read?

WILL: Piss off.

NED: Are you trying to get away from us?

WILL: I'm already away from you.

NED: Escape? Is that why you read?

WILL: I read because I write. It is a necessity of the trade.

NED: Fascinating. And do you write because you read?

WILL: Stop that!

NED: I just wondered ... *(He lays a finger on the open book and reads aloud.)* "... she received a whole succession of letters from him, begging her to visit him, but she treated him with such disdain ..."

(WILL snaps the book shut in exasperation. NED takes it from him and, finding the place, goes on reading.)

"... she treated him with such disdain, that when she finally appeared it was as if she mocked him ..." Are you still going on about this?

WILL: Yes. And will until I get it right.

NED: Liar. You could write it in your sleep. You're just afraid of it— thank God. *(Referring to the book.)* What is this?

WILL: Plutarch.

NED: *(Reading.)* "... she came sailing up the river in a barge with a poop of beaten gold—its purple sails all billowed in the wind ..."

(WILL attempts to retrieve the book. NED evades him.)

"... and while she languished, her oarsmen kissed the water with their oars of silver ..."

MATT: She? What "she" is this? Sounds like Gloriana, going down the Thames to Essex House.

(MATT removes his tunic and starts to wash off his make-up.)

JACK: It's Cleopatra going down the Nile to Antony.

(WILL lunges for the book and gets it.)

WILL: Thank you.

(He puts the book in his pocket.)

MATT: What's the big secret? Come on—spill it!

JACK: *(Starting to wash away his make-up.)* The big secret is, our playwright has begun to fashion the tale of Antony and Cleopatra, but doesn't dare "finish" it. Too reminiscent of a recent love story ... and too dangerous.

WILL: Leave it.

JACK: Too reminiscent of a certain passion ... coming to a headless end tomorrow.

WILL: Leave it.

JACK: Too near the Queen's heart for telling. And perhaps his own ...

WILL: Leave it!

JACK: *(To MATT.)* It's me and Ned he wants to write it for. I wish he'd finish it.

NED: I won't be here to play it.

WILL: Don't say that, you cheap dramatic slut! Don't play your death! Live it! Damn you.

NED: So—are you going to save me? Doctor Shakespeare and his magic cure!

HARRY: Please, Ned. Don't.

NED: Don't, yourself—my pretty rutting maid! Keep your bloody concerns to yourself.

HARRY: I only ...

NED: It's my death, Harry. Mine! Leave me to it. *All* of you!

LUDDY: *(Off—roaring.)*
But when I come to man's estate,
With heigh-ho, the wind and the rain,
'Gainst knaves and thieves men shut their gate,
For the rain it raineth every day.

Scene Three

(LUDDY BEDDOES, one of the company's character men, is manhandled into the barn by two young men. LUDDY is costumed for the role of Friar Francis in Much Ado. *He continues to sing while the others talk.)*

FIRST MAN: There you go, then. And stay there.

SECOND MAN: *(To all.)* Mind you *all* stay. There's a curfew and the Watch has dogs. If you value your heels, you won't go running.

FIRST MAN: Pah! Actors! Drunken louts, the lot o'them ...

(The two men exit.)

MATT: So you got left behind like us, did you?

LUDDY: It's getting cold out there.

MATT: I thought you'd be on your way to Cheapside by now.

LUDDY: Somebody put up the fire.

NED: Put it up your ... self.

LUDDY: Can't. Me hands is too cold.

(HARRY takes fuel from the basket and feeds the brazier. LUDDY moves down to take advantage of its warmth.)

WILL: I see. They caught you seducing another battalion of women— is that it?

LUDDY: Well, I just been taking advantage of my apparel, that's all. Oh—these country kitchen-girls! I told this lass—"there's such a thing as Friar's Rights, you know." I said: "You never heard tell of Friar's Rights? Why," I said, "the Bishop shall hear of this, and he'll set you a penance!" "Oh," she says, quaking, "oh," she says. "I never knew. Don't tell." "Well," I said, "well, seeing as how you repent," I said, "you might do your penance here and now. After all," I said, "isn't it Shrove Tuesday—a day set down for penance?" And she said, "What penance might that be, sir?" And I said, "Penance comes by numbers, child ..." *(He cups imaginary breasts.)* "... two of these, and one of these." *(He gropes himself.)* And then I said, "there's a room 'neath the stair, just there—a closet full of linen for the table. Pure white linen—a suitable bed for a penance." And off she came with me, just like a lamb! A perfect triumph. "Friar's Rights!" Oooh! I pray you, Master Will, that I should play the Friar more often. Small parts have large rewards.

WILL: I don't want to know about your *rutting* parts.

LUDDY: Oh, now, Master Will ...

NED: I was taken once, beneath a stair.

LUDDY: And was there linen?

NED: No. It was done standing up. By the man who had me first ...

LUDDY: What—your father?

(NED strikes him. LUDDY lunges, but others restrain him.)

Here, now!

NED: You ... You filthy ... You god-damned filthy old man. I hope to Christ she poxed you.

LUDDY: It's you that's poxed, my lad! It's you that's patched with the pox! You that's got running sores of the pox! Not me! Not me! I wouldn't touch a boy—nor a *man*—not if you put me on the rack! You, with it up your arse! Or your own up someone else's! If you'd put it where it belongs, it wouldn't have killed you!

(The BEAR calls, off.)

JACK: Be quiet, Luddy.

LUDDY: Calling me a filthy old man—and him a whore!

JACK: Be quiet.

LUDDY: A person ought not appear on a public stage with the likes of you, Ned Lowenscroft.

NED: Then why don't you quit, you fiddling old fart.
>   *(The BEAR calls off.*
>   *He begins to exit upstage.)*
>   I'm going to feed the bear.
>   *(NED exits.)*

HARRY: *(To LUDDY, on the verge of tears.)* You bastard.

LUDDY: That's right—defend him. Kiss his bleeding arse.

HARRY: But—he's dying, for Christ's sake! *Shut up!*

JACK: Come on, you two. Calm down. Luddy, Drink some ale.

LUDDY: I only meant to tell a good story ... I thought *Friar's Rights* was funny as hell. But I'm not a filthy old man.

PERCY: Of course not. You're not even sixty yet!

WILL: *(To HARRY.)* You all right?

HARRY: Yes. I guess. He says that bear's the only friend he has.

WILL: Well, we know that isn't true. Don't we.

HARRY: He won't let me touch him, Will. "Pox," he says. "The pox." Pushes you away, as if he didn't want a friend.

WILL: He played a Beatrice this afternoon, the likes of which we may never see again.

HARRY: Ned can play anything—

WILL: Except his own life, damn him.

HARRY: He saved that bear! No one else would have done that. Only Ned. I *saw* him. Got right down and saved it from the pit—the dogs. Near dead, it was.

WILL: I believe you, but—

HARRY: But if a bear can be saved—why not Ned?
>   *(There is distant music for a formal dance.)*

PERCY: I was a dancer once. All the courtly dances ... Come along, Ben, you'll have to do this one day—and do it right!
>   *(PERCY plays the Lady, teaching BEN the dance.)*
>   Ta dum ... ta dum ... ta *dum!*
>   *(WILL sits in the prince's chair, takes out his pencil and note-book, and starts to write.)*

Scene Four

(LADY MARY STANLEY appears in the barnyard, cloaked and hooded. She carries a lantern. The dancing continues until LUDDY sees her.)

LUDDY: 'Ere, 'ere. Who might this be?

STANLEY: Gentlemen ...

MATT: Madam?

STANLEY: Are you what remains of the Lord Chamberlain's Men?

MATT: We are. The others escaped ...

(WILL kisses the notebook and pockets it.)

STANLEY: So, you have been told about the curfew.

LUDDY: Aye ... for fear the people will rise in Essex's behalf.

MATT: What might we do for you, madam?

STANLEY: Have you a chair?

MATT: A chair? *(To LUDDY.)* Have we a chair?

LUDDY: *(To PERCY.)* Have we a chair?

PERCY: *(Hurrying down to WILL.)* Have we a chair?

(WILL rises, revealing the prince's chair.)

WILL: A chair.

PERCY: *(Decisively.)* Yes. *(He hurries back to LUDDY.)* We have a chair.

LUDDY: *(To MATT.)* We have a chair.

MATT: *(To STANLEY.)* Yes, madam. We have a chair.

STANLEY: What sort of chair?

MATT: *(To LUDDY.)* What sort of chair?

LUDDY: *(To PERCY.)* What sort of chair?

PERCY: *(Hurrying to WILL.)* What sort of chair?

WILL: This sort of chair. Take it and show her.

(PERCY turns and calls back to LUDDY.)

PERCY: Take it and show her ...

TOM and BEN: *(Together.)* Take it and show her!

WILL: *(Pulling at PERCY's arm.)* You take it and show her.

PERCY: Yes. Yes. Of course. Me. I'll take it ...

(He picks up the chair and starts upstage with it.)

I haven't had this much business to do in a dog's years!

(He carries the chair up to STANLEY and sets it down with a flourish.)

Madam—the chair.

OTHERS: The chair!

STANLEY: *(To MATT.)* Have you a cushion?

MATT: *(To LUDDY.)* Have we a cushion?

LUDDY: *(To PERCY.)* Have we a cushion?

PERCY: *(Blankly.)* Have we a cushion ...

(He turns, but WILL cuts him off.)

WILL: Yes.

PERCY: We do?

WILL: There's a bum-roll up Harry's skirts. That should be cushion enough for anyone.

HARRY: My bum-roll?

WILL: Yes. Take it off.

(WILL lifts HARRY's skirts, revealing his bourrelet.)

HARRY: *(Untying the bow.)* I only kept it on to keep me warm ... It's mine and I want it back.

(WILL carries it to STANLEY.)

WILL: There. It is the curse of men's bodies, madam, not to have hips. For the playing of women, this is worn.

STANLEY: *(To HARRY.)* Was it you who played the Lady Hero this afternoon?

WILL: Yes. That's Harry Pearle.

STANLEY: You were charming, Master Pearle. And I thank you for your ... your hips.

HARRY: You're welcome.

STANLEY: Yes. This will do nicely. Thank you. *(To MATT.)* Have it put in the chair, and the chair down by the brazier.

(MATT does so.)

WILL: Why, Madam?

STANLEY: Because, sir, we are coming in.

(She exits into the courtyard.)

MATT: Does anyone know who she is?

WILL: Presumably, one of the Court ladies.

MATT: A truant lady, in that case. Shouldn't she be with the Queen?

LUDDY: Who cares where she ought to be. She's coming in here!

(He finds a mirror and begins to correct his appearance.)

PERCY: I doubt she'll be interested in the likes of you.

LUDDY: More likely me than you, old man. Jesu! Make way for the life of an actor! We are notorious! Even the Court ladies seek us out. Who would stay with the dowdy old Queen, knowing *we're* out here in the barn! Not me, I wouldn't.

(STANLEY returns, preceded by two hooded women.)

Dowdy old Queen and her crazy vigil. Downright bloodthirsty, that's what it is. Imagine! To cut off your lover's head! Lover—ex-lover—whatever. *Reprobate* lover! That's it! He tried to bring her down from her throne and ...

(The women enter and make their way to the chair.)

Here, here! *(To JACK.)* Three of 'em!

(He steps forward.)

STANLEY: Thank you. No. *(Pause.)* Madam.

(She indicates the chair to one of the hooded women. The woman sits, pulling aside the skirts of her cloak. A foot is offered, wearing a boot, which STANLEY removes and sets aside. The second foot is offered, and its boot removed. STANLEY replaces the boots with brocade slippers. The woman draws back her hood. All the men except WILL fall to their knees. WILL bows his head.)

ELIZABETH: What hour is it?

STANLEY: Not yet ten, Madam.

ELIZABETH: Up—up. Enough amazement. Give me some drink. I am dry.

JACK: There is nothing but ale, Your Majesty.

ELIZABETH: Then ale is what I want. *Now.*

(HARRY draws a tankard of ale from the keg. ELIZABETH stares at JACK. JACK stares back.)

ELIZABETH: *(To JACK.)* And you, sir? You are ...?

JACK: You saw me this afternoon, Majesty. I was Benedick.

ELIZABETH: You stare as though you had never seen a woman you could not have.

HARRY: *(Handing her the tankard.)* Madam.

ELIZABETH: And you?

HARRY: I was Hero, Madam.

ELIZABETH: Your health, Master …?

HARRY: Pearle. Henry Pearle, Your Majesty.

> *(He curtsies.)*

ELIZABETH: You curtsy by instinct, Master Pearle?

HARRY: No, Madam. By habit. It is the gown that curtsies.

ELIZABETH: Very nicely said. And who else is here? Have we Master Shakespeare?

WILL: Yes, Majesty.

ELIZABETH: I enjoyed your play. To the extreme.

WILL: Madam.

ELIZABETH: I especially liked the character of Beatrice. I have much sympathy with her.

WILL: Madam.

ELIZABETH: There was a song I liked. "Sigh no more." It suited my mood. And Beatrice had a line …

> *(STANLEY whispers to her.)*

"I will live a bachelor." That suited me, too. I must tell you, Master Shakespeare, I liked her better before she was joined to the Benedick.

WILL: Yes. And was easier to write …

ELIZABETH: More wit, than once she was joined with him. Yes?

WILL: Yes. Indeed.

ELIZABETH: When my sex is joined with yours, whatever else we lose, we also lose our wit.

> *(She loosens her cloak, revealing a white dress and ropes of pearls.)*

I have come here to be in your company, Master Shakespeare. I require distraction. And I warn you—I shall keep as many of you as I can on your feet till dawn.

WILL: Madam.

> *(The third woman, the elderly COUNTESS of HENSLOWE, lowers her hood.)*

ELIZABETH: Will none of you gentlemen help these ladies from their boots?

> *(MATT steps forward and as he kneels before STANLEY, it is clear that she is attracted to him. Looking up, he catches her staring—and reciprocates. She hands him slippers, drawn from*

a pocket inside her cloak. BEN removes HENSLOWE's boots— while she, being old, supports herself on a cane.)

I love a barn. I've always felt safe in a barn. Because of the animals, no doubt. All the animals in a barn are benign—excepting the bull and the boar. *(She looks pointedly at LUDDY.)* One must be wary of them. But—I love the smell of horses, cattle—hay. Such a warm safe place. I trust that you are comfortable.

WILL: Yes. Yes. Absolutely.

JACK: Just like home.

ELIZABETH: And you lads there—well played—and pretty faces.

PERCY: I was a boy once, too. One of the Children's Players of the Chapel Royal.

ELIZABETH: And played the boy's part?

PERCY: No, Madam. I played the lass. Men sent me flowers … *parcels* of them …

JACK: Not again, Percy. Not again.

ELIZABETH: I dare say I might have seen you, Master Gower.

PERCY: She knows my name!

ELIZABETH: But of course I do. Percy Gower was a clown of great repute, many years gone. I remember you for your exquisite falling down.

(She begins to wander the stage, lifting up properties and bits of costume, exploring them at random.)

PERCY: *Exquisite.* Oh, Madam. *My exquisite falling down!* You hear that? Of course, it's true I fell down with much style. A proper tumbling fall, I had. And was famous for it. Also, for my dancing.

ELIZABETH: I do not recall your dancing.

PERCY: Oh, but that was in my lady-days—in skirts.

(ELIZABETH holds Ned's discarded gown against her, and gives its skirts a kick.)

ELIZABETH: In my *lady-days*, I was a dancer, too, Master Gower. I was a dancer, too. Tra-la!

(She tries to dance.)

I've spilt my ale on this pretty gown.

WILL: No harm done, Madam.

(He turns away, furious—the cost!

ELIZABETH holds out her tankard at arm's length. STANLEY takes it and passes it to HARRY.)

STANLEY: More.

HARRY: *(Tankard to LUDDY.)* More.

LUDDY: *(Heading for the keg.)* More ...

PERCY: *(Snatching the tankard.)* Mine! *(Embarrassed.)* My turn ...
(He draws ale and carries it to ELIZABETH.)

ELIZABETH: This gown was on your Beatrice, this afternoon, Master Shakespeare. When she mourned the death of Hero.

WILL: Yes.

ELIZABETH: And worn with grace. I wish I were an actor.

WILL: There are those who claim you are, Madam.

ELIZABETH: What? A *man*?

WILL: No, Your Grace. But one who performs with great skill.
(PERCY arrives with the ale, which she exchanges for the gown.)

ELIZABETH: "I cannot be a man with wishing, therefore ..." What is the rest of that?

WILL: "I cannot be a man with wishing, therefore, I will die a woman with grieving."

ELIZABETH: "I cannot be a man with wishing—therefore I will die a woman." *(She toasts WILL.)*

WILL: "... with grieving."

ELIZABETH: I did not mean to say *with grieving!* I will not grieve! No grieving. None.
(HENSLOWE wavers.)
Someone bring the Countess to a stool, a chair, a bench ... whatever. She is old.
(TOM brings a folding chair. HENSLOWE sits.)
Dearest Anne, it is not I who makes the night. Forgive.

HENSLOWE: Madam, there is no need.

ELIZABETH: You have stayed beside me all my life. If any of you gentlemen require a lesson in loyalty, look to Anne, Countess of Henslowe. By example, she is all you need to know.
(The bell tolls. All listen.)
Ten o'clock. Nine hours remaining ... in this watch.
(The distant music begins an excessively sedate dance tune.)
I want brighter music than that. One of you go and say so.
(LUDDY starts away.)

Not you, Friar. They would not believe a friar had come from me. No. Master Edmund—you shall go. They will believe the Queen has sent them Benedick.

(JACK grabs his scarlet tunic and puts it on as he starts away.)

You have not yet received my permission, sir.

JACK: Madam?

ELIZABETH: Your back, sir, has *impudence* written on it.

JACK: My apologies.

ELIZABETH: I trust it is not written on your face. *Look at me, sir!!*

(JACK turns. ELIZABETH is shaken by his resemblance to Essex.)

Are those your true colours?

JACK: No, madam. But they'll be useful in the Court.

ELIZABETH: Your eyes—what colour are they?

JACK: Blue.

ELIZABETH: Blue. Yes. Blue. They would be, wouldn't they.

JACK: Your Grace?

ELIZABETH: All Irishmen have blue eyes. And … You may go.

(He does not.)

You may—*go*—sir.

JACK: Madam.

(He exits through courtyard.

TARDY enters from up left with an armful of damaged costumes, still wearing her spectacles on her cap. She dumps the costumes upstage.)

TARDY: If you lads is interested, there's a gutter back there for the horses. Makes a good latrine for a man standing. Not for ladies. I said to this large white mare, I said: if I beg your pardon, Missus, do you mind if I use your straw for lady-matters? And she says: neigh! *(She laughs and begins to exit up left.)* Neigh, she said! You can have that one, Master Will, if it pleases you …

(She exits.

ELIZABETH laughs.

The dogs bark.

The WATCH escorts JACK back to the doors.)

JACK: Madam—the dogs …

ELIZABETH: *(Turning.)* Are you the Watch?

WATCH: Madam.

ELIZABETH: He takes a message from the Queen. Let him pass.

WATCH: Your Majesty.

> *(The WATCH and JACK exit.*
>
> *TARDY re-enters from up left, now carrying a sewing basket and a hat. She is oblivious of the new arrivals.)*

TARDY: What is it you lads do to these poor hats? Squished all down round the crown—their innards gutted. Worse than if a fowler had been at them! And still my specs lost.

> *(TARDY comes to ELIZABETH, who cautions the others to silence. TARDY stares at the Queen's gown and fingers its sleeves— peering at them closely.)*

Here! Who said you could wear that? That's my best Lady Capulet, I warrant. You aren't to traipse around in that! So. Which one are you? Got up like that, I wouldn't know you.

> *(She touches ELIZABETH's face.)*

You Master Ned, playing your games on Tardy again? He's always doing that. Dressing up for the wrong play. Master Saucy!

ELIZABETH: What is your name, madam?

TARDY: Here. Whose voice is that?

ELIZABETH: It is me, madam. *I.*

TARDY: Mercy—you don't half do it well … The hair's a wonder. And them pearls …

> *(ELIZABETH smiles and lowers the spectacles onto TARDY's nose. TARDY steps back.)*

Lord love us! You mean I put my hands on the Queen?

ELIZABETH: Indeed.

TARDY: Oh—that I should ever wash them off. These hands were on the Queen's own person. You ought not to have let me, madam.

ELIZABETH: Tell me your name.

TARDY: Kate, Your Majesty. Kate Tardwell.

ELIZABETH: Are you really blind as you seem?

TARDY: Lord, madam—I'm blind *because* I seam! These that I have are *seamstress-eyes.*

> *(ELIZABETH laughs.)*

Got over many years of tiny stitching. I can still find my way with a needle, mind you. It's the world at large that confounds me.

ELIZABETH: It confounds us all.

TARDY: *(Indicating WILL.)* Not him, it don't. He sorts the world the way I sort my threads—unravels it—and sews it back together. Same as he sews his people.

(She takes a stool and sits near lantern light, setting her basket beside her.)

ELIZABETH: There's a commendation for you, Master Shakespeare. A tailor of lives, is that it?

WILL: Perhaps. But it takes an actor to wear them.

(ELIZABETH holds up a scarlet tunic, taken from the pile of clothes that need mending.)

ELIZABETH: Benedick wears one like this. And Claudio.

WILL: Captains' tunics. Yes.

ELIZABETH: Worn for the wars, is that it? Scarlet to bleed in, Master Shakespeare? How blunt of you. How unsubtle. Your Benedick— your Claudio—they almost seem to be platonic lovers. I distinctly caught an echo of my Lords now resting in the Tower. Was this intentional?

WILL: Not intentional. Circumstantial. All soldiers tend to love their comrades.

ELIZABETH: Not to say *worship*. You, that were Claudio—bring your tunic here.

(MATT does so. STANLEY watches him.)

TARDY: There's one of them tore already. Don't you go spoiling the other.

ELIZABETH: *(To MATT.)* Hold it up.

(Each holds up a scarlet tunic.)

There. You see? The very shape and colour of two headless men. No love between them, now—no bonding of allegiance—riding into the streets—raising their swords—*against their Queen.*

(ELIZABETH snatches MATT's tunic away from him.)

TARDY: Here! Mind them!

ELIZABETH: *(To WILL.)* I think this one belongs to you. Take it as a memento of Southampton—he that was your patron.

WILL: Madam ...

ELIZABETH: Were you invited to speak?

(ELIZABETH puts her hands into her tunic's arms.)

I wore such a man ... once.

(She extracts her arms.

Beyond the courtyard, the dogs bark.)

Scene Five

ELIZABETH: *(To LUDDY)* Friar?

LUDDY: Oh. That's me. Yes.

ELIZABETH: Why did you call my Lord Essex a reprobate?

LUDDY: Did I?

ELIZABETH: "Her lover—ex-lover. Her reprobate lover …" You were not reciting lines. I know a rehearsal of lines when I hear one. They speak by rote in Council every day. *Her reprobate lover!!* I think you do not know the meaning of the word.

LUDDY: Oh—oh—madam …

ELIZABETH: I also think I saw you play the part of Falstaff, once. The word describes him perfectly. Debauched! Crapulous! Licentious! Dissolute! Swinish! Hoggish! *Bestial!* Would the Queen invest her love in such a man? Would she?

LUDDY: Madam—Majesty—Your Grace—I meant no more than …

ELIZABETH: No more than what?

LUDDY: Than to express the … the people's view … their horror at his sedition …

ELIZABETH: The people love him! Worship him! Have you never heard him praised? For his courage—for his stature—for his beauty?

LUDDY: No. No, Madam. No. He was … he was … he *is* a traitor!

ELIZABETH: Not *reprobate.* Learn your language. The word you seek is *ingrate. Ingrate!* A word with which every man is imbued—and every woman, familiar. Go.

LUDDY: Madam?

ELIZABETH: Go! You look like my father risen from the grave … And you argue like a weathercock. You shall not gain my favour. Take yourself to bed … *(She sees PERCY.)* … and Master Gower, too.

LUDDY: Take him to his … bed?

ELIZABETH: Now.

LUDDY: Treating us like children.

WILL: Yes—and why not?

ELIZABETH: Yes—and why not. *(To TARDY.)* And those lads, too— they should be abed.

TARDY: Madam ...

(TARDY gathers BEN and TOM. Meanwhile, LUDDY prods PERCY.)

PERCY: Who's that?

LUDDY: Me. And keep your hands to yourself.

PERCY: I was having such a naughty dream.

LUDDY: Yes—well. You can keep your naughty dreams to yourself.

PERCY: "Jesu! Jesu! The nights that I have spent!"

(PERCY and LUDDY, using the ladder, exit into the loft, where we see them settle into the hay. TOM and BEN begin to exit with TARDY.)

ELIZABETH: *(To BEN.)* And where will you sleep in this barn?

TARDY: There's a hay rick yonder, Your Majesty. I'll see them safely to bed.

ELIZABETH: Go with your 'tire mistress, then. Go on.

(The three of them exit up left.

ELIZABETH moves to where HENSLOWE is sleeping.)

See how life bends us, Master Shakespeare. To live. To be—until we become entirely who we are—a bent old woman sleeping in a chair ...

(She kisses the top of HENSLOWE's head.)

HENSLOWE: *(Waking.)* Oh ... Majesty ... I was dreaming.

ELIZABETH: Sweet dreams, I trust.

HENSLOWE: No, Madam. Horses.

ELIZABETH: *(To WILL.)* Her husband died beneath a horse. It fell. In the hunt ...

HENSLOWE: Down it went—and him beneath it. In my dreams, he is always there. In my dreams, I am always young. In my dreams, I have not aged a single year since he died. How can one so young be so old? Every morning, the mirror lies ...

(The distant music begins again—with a lighter touch.)

Good. That's better music. Perhaps now that damned Irishman will return.

(ELIZABETH holds out her tankard to STANLEY, who goes for ale. Meanwhile, NED enters up left, leading the BEAR by a chain. ELIZABETH does not see them.)

STANLEY: Madam ...

ELIZABETH: *(Listening to the music.)* Be still.

STANLEY: But, Your Grace ...

ELIZABETH: I have asked for *silence!!*

NED: *(A bit tipsy.)* Who the rutting hell is that?

ELIZABETH: *Silence!*

NED: *(To the BEAR.)* Luddy's brought in the fishmonger's daughter ...

STANLEY: *Sir!!* How dare you!

NED: Oh, dear—a pair of 'em! Two bawds, *braying.*

> *(He "brays," and then sings.)*
> Two bawds went a-braying, O!
> Two bawds went a-braying!
> Two braying bawds for laying! O!
> Two bawds went—

WILL: Ned. Tarry, sweet Beatrice.

> *(NED turns, sees ELIZABETH and falls down .)*

NED: Dear Jesus Christ! Oh, dear Jesus Christ!

ELIZABETH: Why is the Lady Beatrice lying on her face?

> *(The BEAR stands up and ambles down towards NED.)*

STANLEY: Oh—oh—Madam.

ELIZABETH: Has someone brought me a bear? Did I ask for a bear?

STANLEY: No, Madam.

ELIZABETH: Is he dangerous?

WILL: Not at all. He's quite well tamed.

ELIZABETH: Is he yours?

WILL: He belongs to Master Lowenscroft.

ELIZABETH: Beatrice has a bear! Wonderful! May one approach him?

WILL: Yes.

HARRY: Ned sleeps with him.

ELIZABETH: In a bed?

HARRY: Oh, yes. In the bear's arms. Here, they've been sleeping behind bars in the granary—so's the bear won't frighten the horses—nor the dogs get near the bear.

ELIZABETH: Good bear. Sweet bear.

> *(The BEAR stands and "speaks." ELIZABETH caresses his head.)*

Master Lowenscroft, get up. I want an introduction to your bear. Has he a name?

NED: Harry.

ELIZABETH: I can't hear you.

WILL: Harry, Madam. He said *Harry.*

ELIZABETH: Shush. I want to hear it from him. From Beatrice.

WILL: Get up, Ned.

NED: Can't.

ELIZABETH: Rise!

(NED rises.)

And the dear bear's name?

NED: Harry. *(Mischief occurs to him. He smiles.)* Harry Wriothesley.

ELIZABETH: *(To WILL.)* Your Harry, then. Southampton that is in the Tower with Essex.

NED: Some would have him brought from the Tower.

ELIZABETH: And some would not. He plotted against me.

NED: Not against the Queen. Only for Lord Essex.

WILL: Ned ...

ELIZABETH: And what has Southampton's name to do with bears?

NED: The bear was baited, Madam. Almost to death, by dogs. Everyone crying for his blood. I bought him from the keeper. Bears should go free.

ELIZABETH: You think Southampton is bear-like, Master Lowenscroft? Or merely baited.

NED: Baited.

ELIZABETH: By me? Or by circumstance ...

NED: Circumstance didn't put him in the Tower.

ELIZABETH: The Law Towered him. The Law ... his peers.

NED: And if his peers had set him free, what would you have done then? Concur? Or sent them all to the Tower for their lack of judgment.

ELIZABETH: You have a great deal to say, for a woman.

NED: Yes. But I can shed *my* woman. *(He removes his cloak, revealing tights and a long white shirt.)* Here today—and gone tomorrow.

ELIZABETH: Your impertinence may be charming, Master Lowenscroft. It may also destroy you.

NED: I'm already destroyed.

ELIZABETH: Oh?

NED: The pox. As you can see ...

ELIZABETH: We are all poxed, Master Lowenscroft—one way or another. Life is a pox. It leaves its scars on all of us.

NED: This pox kills, Madam.

ELIZABETH: Life kills. That is its purpose. Have you ever played the part of a Queen, Master Lowenscroft?

NED: In *The Tragedy of King Richard the Third,* I played King Henry's widow.

ELIZABETH: Margaret, then.

NED: Yes.

"Can curses pierce the clouds and enter heaven?
Why, then—give way dull clouds to my quick curses!
Long die thy happy days before thy death;
And after many lengthened hours of grief,
Die neither mother, wife, nor England's queen!"

(Absolute silence.)

Unquote. *(He curtsies and rises.)* I also play Titania—*Queen of the Fairies!*

(He "swishes" past ELIZABETH and drinks from his jar.)

ELIZABETH: You have an extraordinary candour, Master Lowenscroft. Had you forgot I am your sovereign?

NED: No, Madam. I had forgot I was myself.

ELIZABETH: I admire your honesty. And, this night, I invite you to play whatever you choose. Whatever role—whatever temper. Will that fellow never come back?

WILL: Which fellow is that, Madam?

ELIZABETH: Your Benedick. I forget his name.

WILL: Edmund. Jonathan Edmund.

NED: Oh, he'll never come back. Not our Jack. He's in there bouncing all the ladies of the Court.

ELIZABETH: Bouncing?

NED: Yes, Madam. Bouncing—trouncing—*pouncing!* With a hey, nonny-no—our Jack has gone a-bouncing-oh!

STANLEY: Master Lowenscroft ... The Queen!

NED: The Queen? Has the Queen never bounced? *Bouncing— trouncing, and off with his head!*I thought that's what this was all about.

WILL: Ned.

ELIZABETH: Leave him. He proves an excellent sparring partner— not unlike your other fools.

NED: "Look then to be well edified when the fool delivers the madman."

(WILL moves towards NED.)

ELIZABETH: No, I say. Leave him. Let him be.

(Commotion in the courtyard. Voices—dogs.)

Scene Six

(WILL, MATT, and STANLEY move to protect ELIZABETH. HENSLOWE, who has nodded off, wakes and stands with some effort.)

CECIL: *(Off.)* Call off your dogs, sir! Call off your dogs!

(CECIL enters. Seeing ELIZABETH, he sweeps the floor with his hat.)

Your Majesty.

(The dogs fall silent.)

ELIZABETH: Have you come to give the actors lessons in excess, my Lord? You were told I should not be disturbed.

CECIL: Your Grace—I have been commissioned ... *(Seeing the others.)* Perhaps I should introduce myself ...

ELIZABETH: I know who you are, Pygmy. What is this *commission?*

CECIL: Madam, as Private Secretary to her Majesty, I cannot speak freely before strangers. *(To the others.)* Go.

ELIZABETH: Stay.

CECIL: But, Madam ...

ELIZABETH: They will stay, Pygmy. Come to your commission.

(With elaborate gestures, CECIL begins to loosen his cloak.)

Without all that flamboyance. Just tell me.

CECIL: A petition has been delivered.

ELIZABETH: In whose behalf? *(To MATT.)* Bring me some ale. *(To CECIL.)* In whose behalf?

CECIL: In behalf of the Earl of Southampton, Madam.

ELIZABETH: Oh. *(She looks at WILL.)* You should be interested in this. *(To CECIL.)* From whom?

CECIL: His Countess, Your Grace.

ELIZABETH: Eliza Vernon—damn her. Read it.

CECIL: *(As he seeks more light.)* Oh, Madam! God in heaven! There's a bear!

ELIZABETH: Yes. That's Harry Wriothesley. Why not read your petition to him? It comes from his wife.

CECIL: His *wife?*

ELIZABETH: *(To the BEAR.)* Your Grace, I give you Lord Robert Cecil. Pygmy—Harry. *(To CECIL.)* Get on with it.

CECIL: I ... I ... I ... I ... I ...

ELIZABETH: *Read!*

CECIL: I ... Oh, Madam ... This communiqué was put into my hand for delivery to Your Majesty.

> *(No response.)*

Very well ...

> *(He breaks the seal.)*

(Reading.) "Gracious Sovereign: In addressing Your Majesty on the occasion of my husband's imprisonment, I beg Your Majesty to recall that time when she looked upon my heart as bonded to her own—those happy days when I was Your Majesty's companion ..."

Three "Majesties," Madam!! In a single sentence, Madam! Surely this is excess. I should be very wary, Madam, if I were addressed in such an obsequious manner. *Very* wary, Madam! Three "Majesties"—in the salutation alone!

ELIZABETH: Your definition of *excess*, Pygmy, surprises me, when you gave four "Madams" to three "Majesties."

CECIL: Madam?

NED: Five.

ELIZABETH: Proceed.

CECIL: Uhm ... Yes ... Madam ...

WILL: *(Sotto.)* Six.

CECIL: *(Reading.)* "... I mourn the passing of that happy time with all my heart—as one would mourn the death of happiness itself ..." Oh, Madam. The poor dear child.

ELIZABETH: The "poor dear child" is a common whore. My father would have adored Eliza Vernon. He had a taste for whores. But these were and are my Glories. *(She crosses to STANLEY.)* Eliza Vernon was chosen for her virtue, her grace, her beauty—intelligence—modesty ... *(At MATT.) And her virginity.* This poor child is now the wanton countess *(At WILL.)* of *your* damned Harry! Yes? He ran from your embrace to hers—from your love to hers! Yes—and at your bloody urging! Pregnant! Pregnant! Under my protection—in my dominion—pregnant!

WILL: He married her.

ELIZABETH: Hah! Married! My father married my mother! And after they were married he Towered her! I did the same ... I did the same to my once beloved Eliza—and her husband. Towered. Imprisoned for a pregnancy. They were children. Children! She was ... seventeen. Seventeen. I ... Oh ...

CECIL: Madam ...

(The dogs bark.)

ELIZABETH: Damn him. Damn Southampton! Not a month ago—not three weeks ago, he joined with Essex in their rebellious return from Ireland to steal my crown—my England. Not to say my life!

WILL: No, Madam ... *No.*

ELIZABETH: You vagabond from reality! There were swords in the streets! I pray to God you never get hold of my life and place it at the mercy of your pen! You are incapable of facts. There were swords in the streets—two of them raised by Essex and Southampton. Spare me your histories—your histories are full of lies. *(To STANLEY.)* Mary? Finish this appeal.

(STANLEY takes the letter nervously and reads.)

STANLEY: "In memory of those times, I beg Your Majesty to restore your former love of me. Grant my husband pardon for his deeds. His apparent treachery—his insubordinance were *deviations* only, born of his excessive love of order, and his fear that Your Majesty was being led astray ... by ..." *(Unwilling to say "Lord Robert Cecil.")* "... others of your Court, whose personal ambitions placed Your Majesty's integrity in jeopardy."

(CECIL turns away. WILL watches him.)

ELIZABETH: Finish.

(Seeing STANLEY's distress, WILL takes the letter and reads.)

WILL: "In raising his sword against your Royal person, my husband meant only to bring Your Majesty's attention to this matter. What seemed to be sedition was nothing less than loyalty."

ELIZABETH: *Seemed? Seemed! (She snatches the letter.)* That sword Southampton raised was not a *seeming* sword. Nor was it a *seeming* alliance he formed with Essex! Seemed! Seemed! I will give you *seemed*. Pygmy! Take this page and burn it!

(CECIL takes the letter with a smile, crosses to a lantern, and inserts the letter until it catches fire, throwing the residue into the bucket.)

CECIL: Done.

ELIZABETH: In your play this afternoon, Master Shakespeare, there was a line I shall never forget—a sentiment crystallized in two short words. I know you will know which words I mean. Say them—and bring this moment to a close.

WILL: No, Madam. I—

NED: "Kill Claudio."

ELIZABETH: Thank you.

Scene Seven

ELIZABETH: *(To WILL.)* You are too forgiving. You spared him. Claudio. For all his villainy—for all his willingness to believe the worst of that poor girl, you spared him. *(To MATT.)* You—you played that devil—am I right? Claudio?

MATT: I did.

ELIZABETH: You should be drawn and quartered.

MATT: It was only a play, Madam.

ELIZABETH: Oh, yes. Yes. *Only a play.* Just as Southampton would have us believe. He merely *played* the villain. *(To WILL.)* Were you lovers?

WILL: Madam?

ELIZABETH: Lovers. You and Harry Wriothesley. I have been given *(She glances at CECIL.)* copies ... anonymous ... of certain poems ...

WILL: Poems?

ELIZABETH: Beautiful, passionate, tender poems—all addressed to a tender, passionate, beautiful young man ...

WILL: There have been many such poems written over time. The Italians excel at them.

ELIZABETH:
"Shall I compare thee to a summer's day?
Thou art more lovely and more temperate ..."

CECIL: Doesn't sound Italian to me.

ELIZABETH: They're credited to you, Master Shakespeare. These poems have your voice. A most distinctive voice. Unique. Were they addressed to him? Southampton? Most poets would be glad to claim them. But then—they were written to a traitor, weren't they.

WILL: Not that I'm aware of. No.

ELIZABETH: I wonder if any such poems have been written for my Lord Essex. Perhaps in Southampton's hand.

WILL: Your Majesty mistakes the nature of their relationship.

ELIZABETH: What? No love poems? Surely you can't believe that. Why, I was told that when Southampton left the Tower—three years ago—on the first occasion of his being imprisoned there, he leapt upon his horse and rode straight off to Essex, leaving his countess in the dust *and* his newborn child! Straight off to Essex!

WILL: Madam ...

ELIZABETH: The sheets must have been so hot, I doubt Essex House stood in need of fires for weeks!

WILL: Madam—

ELIZABETH: *(Shouting.)* Months!! Damn them!! Damn you!! Damn all men—every last one of you!!

NED: Stop shouting!!

(ELIZABETH looks at him—amazed. He smiles.)

You'll frighten the bear.

CECIL: Madam—I am being discourteous here. The Countess Southampton will need some reply. And ...

(The bell starts to strike eleven.)

ELIZABETH: Tell her I said *no*.

CECIL: Indeed—though I must remind Your Grace that—some days ago—Your Majesty gave promise of an audience to the Countess.

ELIZABETH: The promise is broken.

CECIL: But—

ELIZABETH: The promise is broken!

CECIL: *(Deep bow.)* Madam ...

(He exits through the courtyard. The dogs bark. CECIL shouts at them. Silence.

NED, still slightly drunk, has gone to the keg. HARRY joins him when he sees NED can't locate a tankard. ELIZABETH listens to the bell while watching HARRY and NED.)

HARRY: Here, let me.

NED: No. No, damn it. Leave off. Oh, Jesus Christ in heaven! Look at this. I'm bleeding. Blood—running sores. Putrid. And everything itches—everything itches! I will go mad. Oh, God ... What am I going to do? What am I going to do?!

HARRY: Be quiet. Sit down.

(He cleans NED's hand with a wet rag.)

ELIZABETH: *(To WILL.)* So, another hour. *(Pause.)* Is this a love story?

WILL: Yes.

ELIZABETH: Will he die? The Beatrice.

WILL: Yes.

ELIZABETH: Have there been physicians?

WILL: *(Regretting the cost.)* Oh, yes. Every medicine and every torture they can devise. They've burned him with turpentine—purged him with cypress and anointed him with mercury. Nothing changes. No matter how much money, nothing works.

(JACK appears in the doorway. The BEAR moves over to ELIZABETH. She pets it gently.)

ELIZABETH: How did it happen? Does he know who it was?

WILL: A soldier—so he tells it.

ELIZABETH: One of mine?

WILL: Are there others?

ELIZABETH: Of high or low rank?

WILL: He's dead. And best left in peace.

ELIZABETH: Dead of the pox?

JACK: No. Dead of Ireland.

WILL: He died in one of those chance encounters with an Irish bog. We are told he strayed in a moment of panic, after the enemy had pulled him from his horse—and perished. By sinking. He drowned.

ELIZABETH: In Ireland ...

JACK: Yes. In Ireland.

(The dogs bark viciously.

The BEAR stands up and cries out. HARRY crosses and leads him away.)

HARRY: *(Turning.)* It's the dogs, Madam. They remind him of the pit. He forgets he's free.

(HARRY and the BEAR exit.)

Scene Eight

(In the courtyard, there are voices. The dogs quieten. Music is heard—a dance tune full of spirit and gaiety. Two male servants of the royal household enter, carrying a camp table with three small gilt chairs piled on top of it. Two female servants follow, carrying wicker baskets. STANLEY speaks to a male servant, who exits and shortly reappears with three military camp chairs. Meanwhile, STANLEY supervises the unpacking of dishes, goblets, cutlery, food, and wine. A cloth is spread, the table set, candles lit. ELIZABETH concentrates on JACK.)

ELIZABETH: You were such a long time absent, Master Edmund … I trust you were properly entertained.

JACK: I hope this music is more to Your Majesty's liking. I spoke to the musicians, as you charged me.

ELIZABETH: And did you dance, sir?

JACK: Yes.

ELIZABETH: What was her name?

JACK: I danced solo, Madam. I gave them some of my jigs.

ELIZABETH: I see. And nothing else?

JACK: And nothing else.

ELIZABETH: Then what is this?

(She draws a white lace handkerchief from his tunic.)

JACK: I found it.

ELIZABETH: In whose hand?

JACK: In no one's hand, Madam. I found it on the floor.

ELIZABETH: *(Handing him the handkerchief.)* You play the man too well. You even dare lie to the Queen. You may escort me to the table.

(They move towards the table. NED hovers.)

(To NED.) Are you hungry?

NED: No. Thirsty.

ELIZABETH: There is wine here, sir.

(*She sits and gestures for NED to do likewise. NED sits and pours wine.*)

And where in Ireland are you from, Master Edmund?

(*She gestures "sit!"*

JACK pulls out a chair, but remains standing.)

JACK: Dublin, Your Majesty.

ELIZABETH: Dublin. I had thought it a city more enamoured of the Church—of God and of bookish inclination. Is it not the site of your only university?

JACK: Yes, Madam.

ELIZABETH: And yet you rose from it with a sword in your hand.

JACK: I have no sword, Madam.

ELIZABETH: Ah, yes. I still mistake you ...

JACK: It may be you do not, Your Grace.

ELIZABETH: Oh?

JACK: Whatever else I am—I am still an Irish man. And I will not sit with you.

(*He pushes the chair back in place and moves away. Pause.*)

ELIZABETH: Master Lowenscroft? Tell me—would you truly be a woman?

NED: Never.

ELIZABETH: Why? Why would you not be a woman—when you play her with such skill?

NED: I would rather be housed as I am.

ELIZABETH: Housed?

NED: In this ... male flesh.

ELIZABETH: It gives you so much pleasure to be a man?

NED: Did I say it was a pleasure?

ELIZABETH: No. But there was pleasure in your voice.

NED: Then my voice betrays me.

ELIZABETH: If your voice betrays you, it is your voice that tells the truth.

NED: As your voice does, whenever you speak his name.

(*ELIZABETH throws her wine in his face.*)

Ess-ex!! You love him ...

ELIZABETH: I love no one.

NED: Liar.

ELIZABETH: What?

NED: Liar!!

ELIZABETH: *(Enraged.)* You poxed buffoon!!

NED: *(Taunting.)* You overpainted effigy!!

ELIZABETH: *(Screaming.)* I'll have you drawn and quartered!!

NED: *(Roaring.)* You should be stewed in brine!! And pickled!! Kept in jars!!

ELIZABETH: *(Hissing.)* You poisonous—

NED: Poisoned!!

ELIZABETH: —toad!!

NED: Ha!!

ELIZABETH: Hagh!!

NED: Hagh!!

ELIZABETH: You Beatrice in britches!!

NED: And you ... King Hen-er-y in skirts!!

> *(A distant bell is heard—but not chimes. They all listen— sobered.)*

ELIZABETH: The final call for penance ... If tomorrow is to come, we must all be forgiven. And here we are without a priest.

WILL: Might that forgiveness include the Earls of Essex and Southampton?

ELIZABETH: No. God may forgive them their sins, but I will not forgive their treachery.

WILL: But Madam, if God can be merciful, why not the Queen?

ELIZABETH: I cannot be merciful!! It would be the death of England!!

WILL: And if England should die?

ELIZABETH: I might as well not have lived.

WILL: And have you?

ELIZABETH: I killed the woman in my heart, that England might survive ...

WILL: And so—you have already played the murderer ...

ELIZABETH: You! You that fabricated every king of England—and their queens. God knows what you will write of me! I will be a monster under your hand. And I am not a monster.

WILL: Then, what are you? Is it not true you will kill your lover in the morning? And is that not monstrous? You tell me you have killed the woman in your heart … and now you want to kill the man who gave that woman life. Why?

ELIZABETH: Because I love him. And if, because I love him I spare him, I will then have killed the man in me who is England's only defence against her enemies. I will not spare him. Nothing will shake me in this. Nothing. Oh, God. Oh, God … if only I had your capacity for womanhood, Master Lowenscroft. Then at least I could mourn him.

(NED turns away to find his jar—he stays in the shadows and drinks.)

Say it. Tell me what you are thinking, actor.

NED: I am thinking that I am in the Tower with Essex—and that both of us wish there was a safe, dark place where we could hide from death.

ELIZABETH: Your problem is that you have forgotten you're a man. Listen to me. *Listen.* I will strike a bargain with you. If you will teach me how to be a woman … I will teach you how to be a man.

NED: It's too late …

(The bells ring. Midnight.

The lights dim, except on WILL, ELIZABETH, and NED.)

ELIZABETH: No. It is not too late. We are moving from the day of penance into the day of ashes. *(She crosses to the brazier.)* Come here. Kneel down. There.

(She reaches all the way into the brazier.)

WILL: Madam!

ELIZABETH: Be still. *(She dips her fingers into ashes.)* Be still.

(NED kneels beside her. She marks his forehead with ash.)

Qui tollas peccata mundi, miserere nobis; qui tollas peccata mundi, suscipe deprecationem nostrum. Almighty and everlasting God, who hatest nothing that thou hast made … create and make in us new and worthy hearts … *(She smudges her own forehead with ash.)* Will no one say amen?

(WILL looks at them. Slowly, he removes the scholar's cap, goes to the doors, turns for one last look—and exits.

Music.

The last we see is ELIZABETH and NED in a decreasing ghostly light. End of Act One.)

Act Two
Ash Wednesday, 1601

Scene One

(ELIZABETH is seated on a pillow on the floor, writing on a lap desk. NED sits huddled by the brazier. HENSLOWE dozes alone. JACK, MATT, and TARDY have found other places to rest. The table and gilt chairs have been moved to one side. The four servants are seated around the stage. Cold moonlight can be seen.

WILL enters from the courtyard and stands for a moment in the open doorway. He carries the scholar's cap and his notebook.)

WILL: Well—I have seen to my necessities. And more. I have restored the contents of my jar. I would gladly take my jar to the grave, but a man can't bend his elbow in a wooden box.

(The bell chimes four times.)

Four o'clock. Ash Wednesday. And here they are where I left them—all their endings still unwritten. *(He puts on the scholar's cap and refers to the notebook.)* "If you will teach me how to be a woman—I will teach you how to be a man ..." And if that man—that woman—could be found, lives might still be saved ...

(ELIZABETH signals to a servant, who steps forward. She hands over a folded paper. As the servant exits, another servant takes away the lap desk.)

And what was on that page—a life? Or a death? If that letter does not provide a pardon, in just three hours we will hear a cannon fire in that yard out there—the signal that Essex is dead—the last of a relay of cannon fire that will play through London until it crosses the river to us. What then will be the subject of her grief? His death, or her own weakness that she cannot kill without remorse? Let us see which one of these will be the first to break the silence.

(He puts on his cap and begins to write in his notebook.)

ELIZABETH: *(To WILL.)* What are you writing there?

51

WILL: I'd rather not discuss it, Your Grace.

ELIZABETH: But I demand it. I've never seen a writer writing before. How fascinating. Is it your Cleopatra play?

(He closes his notebook.)

WILL: *(Lying.)* Yes, Madam.

ELIZABETH: Are you ashamed of it?

WILL: No.

ELIZABETH: Why, then, must you make a secret of it? Is it scandalous?

WILL: It has its moments.

ELIZABETH: Let me see. *(She takes the book and reads.)* "You play the man too well. You even dare lie to the Queen." But these are my words. Mine. What is this?

WILL: Madam, I am a writer. It is what I do.

ELIZABETH: And I am your subject—is that it?

WILL: No, Majesty. I am your subject.

ELIZABETH: Very clever—though there's nothing new in that. But why am I in this book? Why am I in here? Speak.

WILL: I am attempting to create a monarch, Madam. A monarch's words are of interest to me.

ELIZABETH: *(Regarding a page.)* "Noblest of men, woulds't die? Hast thou no care of me? Shall I abide in this dull world …?" Who is this?

WILL: Cleopatra. When Antony is dying.

ELIZABETH: *(Reading.)* "Hast thou no care of me …?"

NED: *(Reciting, overlapping.)* "Hast thou no care of me? Shall I abide in this dull world, which in thy absence is no better than a sty?"

ELIZABETH: You have this by rote.

NED: Some of it, Majesty. I was to play it, had I lived.

ELIZABETH: *(To WILL.)* Am I your Cleopatra? *(Pause.)* Is your Antony, then, my Essex?

WILL: It had occurred to me.

ELIZABETH: Damn you!

(She throws the notebook at him.

ELIZABETH drifts up to the skips and fingers the black gown worn by NED earlier.)

Scene Two

(TARDY, at the table, takes a bit of food.)

ELIZABETH: Mistress Tardwell.

TARDY: *(Her mouth full.)* Madam?

ELIZABETH: A word with you about this stitching ...

> *(She holds out the black dress. TARDY crosses to her.)*

You mentioned a large white mare ...

TARDY: *(Not understanding her drift.)* Oh yes, Madam. Very large and very white. Queen of the horses—and a wonder. Like yourself.

ELIZABETH: I believe you said you had spoken to her ...

TARDY: I did?

ELIZABETH: Yes. About *lady matters. (She does a subtle "dance.")*

TARDY: Oh! Yes. *Lady matters.* Well! What a density I am. She'd be delighted, I'm sure. Seeing as how she accepted the likes of me, another queen would be more than welcome to share her straw.

ELIZABETH: Thank you.

TARDY: *(Leading ELIZABETH up left.)* Mind you, we mustn't wake them boys. They have all-seeing eyes in the dark ...

> *(As they exit, ELIZABETH sets the gown down. Seconds later, STANLEY enters from the courtyard, does not see ELIZABETH and rushes off, up left. STANLEY returns and picks up the black gown, retreating with it into the barn up left.)*

ELIZABETH: *(Off.)* Where have you been? I want that Beatrice gown—now!!

Scene Three

NED: *(Indicating the notebook.)* What's in there? More of Antony and Cleopatra dying? Nothing you write is complete without a death—is that it? Show it to me.

WILL: It's only notes. But look, if you must.

> *(NED takes the book and flips through the pages.)*

NED: Darkness. It's all about death and darkness. And this! *(He reads.)* "Ah, women, women, look—our lamp is spent. It's out ..." *(Looking around.)* Like hell it is! We have a dozen lamps and I'll light every one. *(He calls out.)* Harry! Every rutting lantern shall be lit!! *(He runs to the up left exit.)* Harry! Harry! Lights! *(He places the notebook in his tights.)*

(*HARRY enters. He now wears only tights and a shirt.*)

HARRY: Are we on fire?

NED: Not yet. Get busy. I want every lantern lit.

PERCY: Every?

NED: Yes! In all the world! Make light. There—those. That one and that one. And that one there.

> (*HARRY begins to light various other lanterns. PERCY and LUDDY climb down and do the same.*)

LUDDY: What's this? Has everyone gone mad?

NED: Yes! Yes! Mad!!

> (*He sings with manic energy.*)
> But let them go,
> And be you blithe and bonny,

ALL: (*Joining in, singing.*)
> Converting all your sounds of woe
> Into hey nonny, nonny!

(*To WILL.*) There aren't any songs in here. There's no one singing.

WILL: There will be ... there will be ...

NED: What?

WILL: Music. Dancing. Feasting ...

NED: Ah! Now—there we have what's missing here. *Feasting.*

WILL: It's Lent, for God's sake.

NED: Not in Egypt!!

> (*All cheer.*)

Harry? Luddy? Bring the table. Bring the chairs.

> (*HARRY and LUDDY start to move the table, MATT and PERCY each start to move a chair, with the servants following with flagons, etc.*)

HENSLOWE: (*Banging the floor with her cane.*) Gentlemen! Gentlemen! Be still!

> (*All freeze and turn toward her. She rises with difficulty.*)

That is Her Majesty's property—and you may not disport it in this fashion. You, sir—put that chair down!

> (*PERCY, with chair raised, does not know what to do.*)

Put it down, sir!

> (*PERCY deposits the chair and meekly sits on it.*)

NED: *(With mock humility.)* Madam, all we have of comfort is Her Majesty's indulgence—this small table—these tiny chairs and this utterly inadequate food—honey cakes and bits of chicken. May we not partake of this repast?

HENSLOWE: Agh! I have no mind for such things any more. There is too much else. Too much else ... *(To others.)* Do as you are asked. I will be deputy. *(To NED.)* And you, sir—I will have wine.

(The others applaud and spring into action. They reprise the last two lines of the song: "Converting all your sounds of woe ..."

WILL finds wine and brings it to HENSLOWE. In the meantime, HENSLOWE's chair is moved, and she is reseated while the table, gilt chairs, and accoutrements are set in place. Servants bring the baskets and set out plates and goblets.)

NED: Now—for our guests.

(He crosses up to the skips and brings two scarlet tunics, setting them out on the backs of chairs. JACK retrieves his tunic from the loft and throws it to NED.)

LUDDY: *(Meanwhile.)* He's gone mad.

PERCY: I seen a man once, walking naked through the streets. Mad as they come. Said he'd been driven from Eden. "Show me the way to go home." Pagh! Them as knew where Eden was would be as mad as he. He was caged and carted soon enough.

(Music.

The lights alter, isolating the table and the chairs.)

Scene Four

(Finished with the tunics, NED spies ELIZABETH about to enter.)

NED: Aha! I could have written this myself. Ladies and Gentlemen! The Queen!

(ELIZABETH enters. HENSLOWE and female servants curtsy, others bow. ELIZABETH now wears the black gown. STANLEY follows, carrying ELIZABETH's white gown, and hands it to TARDY, who has followed her. TOM and BEN enter. NED seats ELIZABETH at the table—after which the others fall back into the shadows.)

ELIZABETH: Since I have chosen to be *with* you, I have elected to be *one* of you. And to that end—*(To NED.)* I am wearing the gown in which your Beatrice mourned the death of Hero.

NED: An interesting choice, Your Grace, given that Hero lived. Are you telling us your hero, too, shall live?

ELIZABETH: Yes. England is my hero. There is no other.

NED: Let us see.

> *(He indicates that WILL should be seated beside the queen and pours wine into their goblets.)*

ELIZABETH: I smell mischief, sir.

NED: Mischief is as mischief does, Madam. *(He smiles.)* Behold!

> *(HENSLOWE sits, and the others settle into comfortable positions and become an audience.)*

Three Captains here ... *(The tunics.)* They are known to all of us. *(He moves to each tunic as he identifies them.)* Yours, Madam. Yours, Sir. And mine.

> *(He holds up the notebook.)*

"Come,

Let's have one other gaudy night: call to me
All my sad captains; fill our bowls once more:
Let's mock the midnight bell."

To the Captains!

ELIZABETH: *(Drinking, mystified.)* Come to the purpose.

NED: Three captains, three stories. Love stories. Yes? To be spoken in front of witnesses.

PERCY: "Then must you speak of three that loved not wisely, but too well ..."

ALL: *(Together.)* Shush!

ELIZABETH: Fool, come and sit near me. I would share your wisdom.

> *(PERCY brings a stool and sits.)*

NED: Let us begin with the Master of Words ... *(To WILL.)* You've had a lot to say about love. As for the thing itself, we know that you have loved—and some of us know it well ...

> *(WILL looks away. ELIZABETH takes note of this.)*

But you wear a mask, thinking that no one can read it. Yet this man here ... *(He lifts the tunic nearest WILL and holds it out)* ... now Towered and despised, now shunned—was once the centre of all your yearning. Is that not so?

> *(NED stands behind WILL, draws the tunic around him like a bib and folds its arms about WILL's neck.)*

Is it not so?

> *(WILL reaches for the arms and lays the tunic in his lap.)*

WILL: Yes.

NED: I can't hear you.

WILL: *Yes!!* Damn you.

NED: *(Reciting.)*
"A woman's face with Nature's soft hand painted
Hast thou, the master-mistress of ..."

I can't remember.

(WILL drapes the tunic on the empty chair's back.)

WILL: *(Reciting.)*
"A woman's face with Nature's own hand painted
Hast thou, the master mistress of my passion;
A woman's gentle heart, but not acquainted
With shifting change, as is false woman's fashion ..."

ELIZABETH: *(To WILL.)* Such a scandalous opinion of women ...

WILL:
"An eye more bright than theirs, less false in rolling,
Gilding the object whereupon it gazeth;
A man in hue, all hues in his controlling,
Which steals men's eyes and women's souls amazeth.

"And for a woman wert thou first created,
Till Nature as she wrought thee fell a-doting,
And by addition me of thee defeated,
By adding one thing to my purpose nothing ..."

(WILL pronounces the final word: "no thing.")

NED: Hah!

WILL:
"But since she prick'd thee out for woman's pleasure,
Mine be thy love, and thy love's use their treasure."

(WILL sits. There is some laughter.)

ELIZABETH: *(Applauding.)* You have a good wit, sir. And the grace to turn it on yourself. Well said.

(The others applaud.)

Mary—more wine.

(She gestures to WILL and NED.

WILL removes the cap.)

STANLEY: Your Grace.

(She exits to the courtyard.)

NED: One thing to *your* purpose nothing? *(Privately, to WILL)* And pigs have wings—is that it? What—*never?*

WILL: *(Possibly lying.)* Never. Not with him.

> *(STANLEY returns with a flagon and a glass for PERCY and begins serving wine.)*

NED: You poor sod. All that love, and nothing for it to feed on. So here you sit, and never had your Captain.

WILL: There are more ways of *having* than one.

NED: Are there, now. Well, whatever ways you mean, they aren't the ways of love I know.

> *(WILL puts the cap on.)*

> *(As STANLEY pours wine.)* Ah, yes—behold the woman. Busy, busy—oh, so lovely. *(To WILL.)* Can you smell her? I can. All that golden-brown hair! And real, no doubt. *(To STANLEY.)* What's it like to play a woman and be one at the same time? Eh? You could give your mistress lessons.

> *(STANLEY slaps him.)*

Ah, no. Too late. She's already given *you* lessons. I could play you—though young Harry there could do it better. The stance is excellent—proud and wary all at once. See that, Harry? The jutting chin—the quivering lip. Don't bite it! No—a brave girl never bites her lip. Harry would never do that. Harry knows better— why don't you? Did Hero bite her lip when she was betrayed? Never.

ELIZABETH: She fainted.

NED: Dead away. Dead. And you, Madam—did you faint when you heard of your lover's betrayal? Ah, no. It would be too *womanly*— and we mustn't have that.

> *(The bell rings five times.*
>
> *Pause.)*

ELIZABETH: Five. Surely not five so soon.

STANLEY: Yes, Madam.

ELIZABETH: Two hours left. Only two. Oh, God … Where is Pygmy? Where is Cecil? Why has he not returned?

NED: Perhaps he has delayed his return for fear that when he comes he will find a woman in your place. Was that not our bargain?

ELIZABETH: Yes …

NED: *(Holding up the notebook.)* Here, Madam, is a description worthy of your Captain. *(Then, sotto voce to WILL.)* The play's the thing, wherein I'll catch the woman in the Queen. *(Now, to ELIZA-*

BETH.) I think it would be fitting if the Queen of England were to read the Queen of Egypt.

(The others applaud.)

ELIZABETH: I warn you—I shall not be ridiculed.

NED: If Madam would but read ...

(He hands her the book.)

ELIZABETH: *(Rising and reading.)*
"His legs bestrid the ocean; his reared arm
Crested the world; his voice was propertied
As all the tuned spheres, and that to friends;
But when he meant to quail and shake the orb,
He was as rattling thunder ..." *(She stops.)*

I do not like this. I will say no more. *(She hands the book to NED. To WILL.)* Essex is not a god! You make him seem like a god! You belittle him with too much praise.

WILL: This is the theatre, Madam, where men play gods every day.

NED: No, Madam. Do not sit. There is more.

ELIZABETH: I said I would say no more.

NED: But the woman, Majesty. Have we not come here for the woman?

ELIZABETH: I no longer know that I want her.

NED: Because you are afraid of her—afraid she will forgive—and pardon.

ELIZABETH: I say I do not like this.

NED: Like it or not—we still await the woman. *(He has found the page he wants and hands her the book.)* I will be your Antony.

ELIZABETH: And what is the occasion? I must know the occasion.

NED: They are parting, Madam. Antony, in Egypt, has been recalled to Rome. His wife has died. Fulvia.

ELIZABETH: It does not interest me.

NED: It should. Cleopatra knows there is a more important reason for his leave-taking.

ELIZABETH: Yes?

NED: Yes. She suspects ... .

WILL: *Knows ...*

NED: Antony is in danger of making an alliance with her enemies.

ELIZABETH: Ireland ...

WILL: Rome.

ELIZABETH: Ireland. This is Essex indeed ... the very same. It is what he did. Precisely.

> *(NED puts on Jack's tunic.)*

WILL: As you say, Madam.

ELIZABETH: As I know. Do not slight my awareness.

NED: And so "... I will leave you, lady."

> *(ELIZABETH does not respond.)*

Majesty? The book ...

ELIZABETH: Yes.

NED: *I will leave you, lady.*

ELIZABETH: *(Reading.)*
"Courteous Lord, one word.
Sir, you and I must part, but that's not it;
Sir, you and I have loved, but there's not it;
That you know well: something it is I would—
O, my oblivion is a very Antony,
And I am all forgotten."

JACK:
"But that your royalty
Holds idleness your subject, I should take you
for idleness itself."

ELIZABETH:
"'Tis sweating labour
To bear such idleness so near the heart
As Cleopatra this. Your honour calls you hence;
Therefore, be deaf to my unpitied folly,
And all the gods go with you ..."

> *(She hesitates.)*

No. I will not say this next. I cannot and I will not be a traitor to myself.

NED: Then, there can be no woman. She says: "Upon your sword sit laurel victory!"

ELIZABETH: How can a woman say that to a man she knows is going to betray her?

NED: Antony *fell* upon his sword. I would call that a victory— wouldn't you?

ELIZABETH: My Lord Essex had ample opportunity to do the same— and did not.

NED: Are you not his sword, Madam? Did he not "fall" on you?

WILL: He tripped.

ELIZABETH: You would make light of any death you had not written.

WILL: Death is death, Madam. It comes—we go.

ELIZABETH: Yet I am here.

WILL: In your time, you too will die. But that is not yet. Not yet.

ELIZABETH: In your reading of me, am I to fall upon my sword?

WILL: In my reading, Madam, you already have.

ELIZABETH: Then you misread me altogether. I shall die of regret.

WILL: For what reason?

ELIZABETH: For never having been myself. Which is more than can be said of Master Lowenscroft, whose only concern is himself. He urges me to be a woman, grieving the death of Essex—when the only death he grieves is his own. *(To NED.)* Where is *your* Captain's death in all of this? I have not yet seen *you* mourn him.

> *(NED takes JACK to the "playing area." JACK lies down and becomes NED's dead captain.)*

NED:
"Noblest of men, wouldst die?
Hast thou no care of me? Shall I abide
In this dull world, which in thy absence is
No better than a sty? O see, my women,
The crown of the earth doth melt. My lord!
O, withered is the garland of the war,
The soldier's pole is fall'n; young boys and girls
Are level now with men; the odds is gone,
And there is nothing left remarkable
Beneath the visiting moon."

> *(All are deeply moved—including NED, who rises and moves away.)*

I saw him first in the yard of Bell's Inn. Six years ago ... I was sitting on the steps—top step leading onto the porches—drinking ale in the sun. *Clatter—clatter*—I can hear it still, the sound of his arrival. His horse was frisky—nervous. When the stable boy came to hold her, my Captain got down and laughed and gave his mare a slap and I heard his voice ...

JACK: "I won't be wanting her till morning, lad ..."

NED: The hair on the back of my neck and all down my arms stood up. He came across the yard—and his boots ... I could hear all the leather on him—smell it. Taste it, almost. He came and looked at me as if I was a curiosity—me staring back like an imbecile.

JACK: "Hello ..."

NED: Hello. And he passed. When I could move, I found him in the tap-room—waiting for me.

JACK: "I'm laying over here, tonight. Will you lay over with me?"

NED: He didn't even ask my name. I knew he was a Captain. That I knew. Everything he said, he took for granted was to be obeyed.

(He picks up the tunic and smells it.)

Nothing, nothing, nothing smells like a man. The smell of his skin, the smell of his hair ...

(He puts on the tunic.)

How was I to know? When I put him on—when I wore him—how could I know? There wasn't a mark—not a single mark of disease on any part of him. Only his wounds and scars—only his soldier-self that had been to the wars and back. But nothing else. Nothing that said *beware—take care.* I never knew such loving—never. Yes. It was rutting. Yes. It was bloody ...

(ELIZABETH puts out her hand towards him. PERCY places his hand on hers.)

Yes. There was hours of it. Hours and hours. All that night—and all the next week. Hours—minutes—seconds. Seconds—minutes—hours. We made love—we sang songs—we ate and drank together ... We told the stories of our lives ... We laughed—we wept—we rejoiced ... I missed a whole week's performances ...

PERCY: We all thought you were dead ...

NED: I was—to everything but life.

(He removes the tunic and puts it back on the chair.)

Then he was gone. *(Beat.)* To Ireland. And one of those endless Irish wars.

ELIZABETH: Ireland. Yes. Where all unhappy stories end ... Did he know?

NED: What? That he had poxed me? Maybe. Maybe not. I only knew there was desperation in him. Panic. But no regret. None.

(Suddenly, he laughs.)

ELIZABETH: What?

NED: At least I bested my mother. All she got of you was a common sailor. My father. But what I got of you was a Captain. And I thank you for him. And for his death. And for my own.

ELIZABETH: *Long live death*—is that it? You are as petulant as Essex in the Tower. You're just another self-centred *boy*. Like him, all you want is someone's everlasting attention.

NED: I'm an actor, Madam.

ELIZABETH: Then play the man!!

NED: I don't know how. It's not my profession.

ELIZABETH: Oh! You are the Prince of Petulance! He could take lessons from you.

NED: May the Prince leave?

ELIZABETH: No. I've not finished. Neither have you. I'm still waiting for the man.

NED: And I am still waiting for the woman.

ELIZABETH: Then you can wait until you rot. She will not be forthcoming. Go. And good riddance.

(NED begins to exit up right. HARRY begins to follow him.)

NED: Stay back.

HARRY: I only ...

NED: Stay back!!

(BEAR cries off.)

Or I will kill you!

(HARRY steps back. NED speaks to ELIZABETH.)

There. Was that man enough for you?

(He exits. ELIZABETH signals to servants to move the table and chairs up stage.)

Scene Five

(WILL removes the scholar's cap.)

ELIZABETH: Master Shakespeare?

WILL: Your Grace.

ELIZABETH: *Is* this a play we are in?

WILL: It would seem so, yes.

ELIZABETH: And what will you call it—this play?

WILL: It can have no name until it is finished.

ELIZABETH: And it will not be finished until my Lord Essex is dead? Is that right?

WILL: Perhaps ...

ELIZABETH: I do not like "perhaps." You enjoy killing?

WILL: Do you?

ELIZABETH: Is Cleopatra's death already written for Master Lowenscroft?

WILL: Yes—but ...

ELIZABETH: He believes he will not live to play it. I wrote a death once. Well written—well played. When Mary Stuart entered the great hall where she would die, *she* was wearing black. And when the black was stripped away, she presented herself in crimson to her executioner. In crimson silks. A great queen—a great actor. Tell Master Lowenscroft: that is how a great queen goes to meet death. Not as its subject—but as its sovereign.

(WILL puts on the scholar's cap.)

Scene Six

ELIZABETH: Mistress Tardwell, have you a glass?

TARDY: Oh, yes, Madam. All actors need a glass. There must be a dozen here.

ELIZABETH: Bring one. And colours. Powder.

(TARDY goes to the skips and rummages. WILL puts his cap back on.)

Mary ...

STANLEY: Majesty?

ELIZABETH: *(Moving to sit in the prince's chair.)* Come and be my woman. Quickly.

(STANLEY kneels before ELIZABETH and takes her hands.)

Child—child. Oh, child. You ... you are so ...

HENSLOWE: *(Attempting to stand.)* I should like to rise.

ELIZABETH: *(To PERCY.)* Fool—help the Countess to her feet.

(PERCY hurries to HENSLOWE and his attempt to get her standing becomes a little dance.)

HENSLOWE: Oh, oh, oh ...

PERCY: Stay. Stay. Stay!

(HENSLOWE falls back. They try again.)

HENSLOWE: Oh, oh, oh. Oh! *Oh!*

PERCY: There now—done.

(TARDY brings a mirror, linen, make-up, and powder to ELIZA-BETH. Servants have already brought a bench to be used as a make-up table.)

TARDY: Here's what we have, Madam. All we lack is a decent red.

PERCY: *(To HENSLOWE.)* Don't move.

(He starts toward the loft.)

TARDY: That Lowenscroft, he used it all in the final act.

PERCY: I have red. *(To HENSLOWE.)* Stay! *(He goes to the loft and retrieves his "Dorothy bag," taking it to ELIZABETH.)* I have here reds to kill. In my lady-days, they would climb up onto the boards and lay their hands on me, as if to drag me down amidst the mob. I used to think: *I will die of wearing red!* But I never gave it up.

HENSLOWE: *(Wavering.)* Oh, oh, oh … .

(PERCY hurries to her.)

I wish to walk.

PERCY: Where, Madam?

HENSLOWE: Anywhere but in the yard. I will not go outside. I have not seen the stars in twenty years, and I do not intend to see them now. Give me your arm.

(She also uses her stick as they commence a walkabout.)

ELIZABETH: I have been myself for so long. These eyes—this mouth … Mistress Tardwell?

TARDY: Madam?

ELIZABETH: Tell me—*anything*—of real life.

TARDY: Your Majesty lives a real life. One can see that. May one say this? Your Grace, you claim to lack a woman. But see here, Madam. *(The mirror.)* There is no woman lacking here. *I* see you. I see you with every breath you take. I, too, have lived your life. One man— another. All are equal in their treachery. *But*—and oh, Madam, if I could give you this—the joy of *one* child. Many died—but one lived. And that child will see me to my death.

ELIZABETH: *(Staring at the mirror.)* Where is Hero? There's a woman.

(HARRY steps forward.)

Look at him, Mary. Your equivalent in every way but one. *(To HARRY.)* What are you most? In there, where you live.

HARRY: Myself.

ELIZABETH: You play the woman so well. How can that be? You're just a boy.

HARRY: I've played the woman all my life.

ELIZABETH: Always the woman? Are you afraid to be a man?

HARRY: I am a man.

ELIZABETH: *(Handing him the mirror.)* Hold this for me so that I can see.

HARRY: In April, I will be nineteen—and then I'll be too old to play in skirts.

ELIZABETH: But, Master Lowenscroft ...

HARRY: When Ned's a hundred, he'll still be the greatest player of women.

ELIZABETH: Mary—my hair.

> *(STANLEY removes ELIZABETH's wig and sets it aside. The QUEEN is bald.)*

So, Master Pearle, you stand amazed. Beneath *your* woman's hair, you say there is a man. Without my woman's hair—must I also be a man?

HARRY: No, Majesty.

ELIZABETH: It pleases me that someone will say so. I cannot bring myself to say it. *(To TARDY.)* More powder, some colour. Hold the glass, boy. *(To STANLEY.)* I should like more wine.

> *(NED enters. He wears a long, white gown over his shirt and tights. It is neither male nor female. He draws ale and stands watching. PERCY reseats HENSLOWE in her chair. She holds out her empty glass. A SERVANT brings wine to them both and to ELIZABETH.)*

Red.

> *(She studies her reflection. She reaches into Percy's "Dorothy bag" and finds a pot of red.)*

When I was first a Queen, I was twenty-five years old. There is much value in youth ...

WILL: But more in age.

ELIZABETH: So you say—but where is the proof of it?

WILL: We are here, Madam.

ELIZABETH: There. Done.

> *(STANLEY moves to put ELIZABETH's wig back on, but is stopped by NED's voice.)*

NED: No. Not done. This is nothing more than Your Majesty playing with colour. Too much white, Madam. Too much red. An actor would know better.

ELIZABETH: *(Rising.)* Would he, now.

NED: To find the woman, Madam, you must hide the man. *Sit.*

(ELIZABETH sits. NED uses the linen gently to wipe away the harshness of what ELIZABETH has created. He leaves both white and red, but modifies them.)

ELIZABETH: Your breath smells of drink.

NED: As does yours. Be still.

HENSLOWE: Master Shakespeare?

WILL: Countess?

HENSLOWE: Who is that young man standing next to Lady Stanley?

WILL: He is an actor, madam. His names is Welles. Matthew Welles. You saw him this afternoon as Claudio.

HENSLOWE: He seems to be uncommonly familiar with the lady.

WILL: Perhaps it will be to her advantage, madam.

HENSLOWE: But—an *actor!* It is scandalous.

WILL: No more scandalous than the Queen's current consort. *(He indicates NED.)* Wouldn't you call his behaviour at this moment uncommonly familiar? Yet the Queen appears to welcome it.

HENSLOWE: Madness. *Actors!* Madness.

(NED has completed his work. Backing away, he takes the Beatrice wig and places it on ELIZABETH's head and holds the mirror for her.)

NED: There, Madam. The complete woman. Such as can be found.

ELIZABETH: But this is Beatrice.

NED: You wanted a woman—I gave you one.

ELIZABETH: One of yours.

NED: No, Madam. One of many.

ELIZABETH: Oh, yes. You have them all at your fingertips.

NED: As you have many men, Madam, at yours.

(ELIZABETH strikes NED. Pause. He goes to his tankard and drinks, his back to ELIZABETH.)

Scene Seven

ELIZABETH: Can nothing provoke you, sir?

NED: Provoke me?

ELIZABETH: A man would strike back.

NED: Would he, now.

ELIZABETH: *Yes!*

NED: To what end?

ELIZABETH: To avenge himself.

NED: Of what? A mere lack of courtesy?

ELIZABETH: I struck you, sir. Reply.

NED: Ah, so. I see. In your woman's guise, you still act the man—and expect me to do likewise. But that's too easy. You want a man? I'll give you a man.

> *(He goes to a skip and rummages. He withdraws an object which he hides behind him. He also draws an unsheathed sword from the skip. With them, he advances on ELIZABETH.*
>
> *The others shout. The BEAR calls, off.)*

STANLEY: Stop!

HARRY, JACK, and MATT: *(Together.)* Ned! Ned! For God's sake!

> *(NED raises the sword. STANLEY screams. NED brings the blade crashing to the floor, and raises the hidden object above him. It is a severed "head" with long dark hair and a gory neck.)*

NED: Here, Majesty, is the only man you need! *God save the Queen!!*

ELIZABETH: Oh, dear Jesus Christ.

> *(She falls to her knees. The others are still. NED lowers the "head" and looks into its face.)*

NED: "O, see, my women … the crown of the earth doth melt." *(He kisses the lips.)* "My lord …"

> *(Hanging the head from a lantern pole, NED crosses downstage, dropping the sword as he passes ELIZABETH, who sags and sits on her hip.)*

ELIZABETH: Get me up.

NED: Get yourself up.

ELIZABETH: *Get me up!!*

> *(Everyone freezes. ELIZABETH reaches for the sword and uses it to push herself up. She advances on NED—raises the sword and brings it down by his side. NED does not move.)*

NED: Next thing we know, your Majesty will seek employment at the Tower. What is your Headsman's name, Madam?

ELIZABETH: What sort of idiot question is that?

NED: What's his name? *History* will want to record it—lest the people think his name was *Elizabeth.*

ELIZABETH: Pah!

NED: Poor old Headsman. Nobody knows his name. Left entirely out of history—not a single mention. I think he deserves a name.

Don't you? Think of it—in the morning—when?—at seven? Two apparently *nameless men* will meet in the courtyard of the Tower. The one whose name you refuse to voice—and the anonymous Headsman. What on earth can history do with that?

ELIZABETH: It can tell the truth.

NED: Which is?

ELIZABETH: That one of them has a name—which you know perfectly well.

NED: Well, no—as a matter of fact, I don't. It's slipped my mind.

ELIZABETH: Essex.

NED: Is that all? Just Essex? Isn't that one of your counties? County Norfolk—County Sussex—County Essex ...

ELIZABETH: Stop it!

NED: What's his *name?*

ELIZABETH: Devereux.

NED: Devereux. A city in France?

ELIZABETH: Stop it!!

NED: Not until I have his name.

ELIZABETH: Robert.

NED: And between the sheets?

ELIZABETH: Oh, God. Make him stop.

NED: There was a time between the sheets—Yes? And whatever happened there—whatever it was—whether everything or nothing—there was a time when he was there with you and you were there with him. And if you cannot mourn that moment, two nameless men *will* meet in the morning and both will be forgotten forever. Madam?

ELIZABETH: Robin.

(She goes to get a drink, and stands with her back to the others.)

NED: I thought I heard a woman there just then. Or something of a woman. That catch in the throat that comes only when speaking a lover's name—Troilus—Romeo—Antony—Robin ...

ELIZABETH: Captain!

NED: Yes—and "Captain."

(The dogs bark.)

ELIZABETH: There is too much woman in you, sir—it seems to me.

NED: Are you daring me to bed you?

HENSLOWE: Master Lowenscroft!

ELIZABETH: Leave him be!

> *(She thrusts her glass at STANLEY.)*

More!

> *(STANLEY fills the glass.)*

Now *you* tell me: *what was his name?*

NED: I don't know.

ELIZABETH: Ah, yes. *It's slipped your mind.* Is that it?

NED: Captain.

ELIZABETH: Is that all? Just *Captain.* Surely between the sheets there must have been more than that. What?

> *(NED turns away.)*

Perhaps he was another Robin—or another Harry. Did you not ask his name?

NED: Yes. Yes—I did.

ELIZABETH: And ...?

NED: He said ... he said his name was ... Hal.

ELIZABETH: What? I didn't hear you.

NED: Hal.

ELIZABETH: My, my. Another Harry, after all.

NED: He did not say *Harry.*

ELIZABETH: No. He said ... *(She whispers.) Hal.* Do you mourn him?

NED: Yes.

ELIZABETH: As a man—or as a woman?

NED: As a man.

ELIZABETH: And yet, you weep.

NED: Men do that, Madam—from time to time.

Scene Eight

ELIZABETH: Tell me the hour. Someone—seek the Watch. He will know. *(To LUDDY.)* You.

> *(LUDDY goes into the yard. Dogs bark.)*

Where is Cecil? What delays him? *Why does he not come?!* Oh, damn the dogs! *Damn them!!*

> *(STANLEY hurries out. The dogs quieten. ELIZABETH sits.)*

We are all in the Tower. Towered. All of us. In this hateful moment.

WILL: If we *were* in the Tower, Madam, lives might be saved.

ELIZABETH: You damn me unfairly. You have the advantage of being unable to pardon. Only I and I alone can pardon. It is a weight you do not bear.

(LUDDY and STANLEY return.)

LUDDY: A quarter from the hour, Madam.

ELIZABETH: Which hour?

LUDDY: Six, Your Majesty.

ELIZABETH: Six. *Oh, where is Cecil!!*

(She sees LUDDY begin to walk away.)

You, sir.

LUDDY: Madam?

ELIZABETH: You remind me of my father.

LUDDY: It is true I have his beard.

ELIZABETH: Also his girth, though he stood better.

(LUDDY laughs nervously and "performs" Henry VIII.)

Whenever I think of the Tower, I think of my father. His breath, like yours, was fouled with food and drink. His hands, like yours, were fat and filthy. He foreswore gloves as being *effeminate.* Besides, his fingers must be free, with so many laces to untie. All women were his—my father's. He was the King. Manhood was his profession.

NED: And yours.

ELIZABETH: No, sir. My name is not Harry. The only skirts I hoist are my own. *(To WILL.)* There was no England in him—only him*self.* Only Harry—only ever Harry. My father. *God,* if I could kill every man in my kingdom, I would do it in a second!! There is *not one* worthy of this moment.

STANLEY: Madam—be at peace.

ELIZABETH: Peace? The world is ending. Even I cannot prevent it. *(To NED.)* Neither can you. You cannot avoid your death any more than Essex can in the Tower. Do what you will, it will come.

NED: No. Not yet.

ELIZABETH: Not yet. *Not yet.* I predict these will be your last words. And will you also say: *I will not go?* Perhaps you could ask Master Shakespeare to write it for you. Another Juliet. Dead—but not dead. *(Beat.)* How will it be? And where?

NED: In a ditch, somewhere.

ELIZABETH: In a ditch? You have no more sense of honour than to find yourself a ditch?

NED: What have I to do with honour?

ELIZABETH: Everything. Look at you, standing there! The greatest actor of women in our time. You have the talent and the body of a god. Pay them your respect. Give them a decent farewell.

NED: I barely know who they are. There's been so little time.

ELIZABETH: But enough to take some joy from them.

NED: Joy, Madam?

ELIZABETH: Joy in your Captain! Joy in your Beatrice! Joy in your comradeship with all these others! To have been so alive! Master Lowenscroft, here we are learning how to go on living—by learning how to die. But to die—even at your age—is not to have failed to have a life. *(She turns to the others.)* Yes?

(The others applaud.

The BEAR enters and "speaks." He has wakened and is looking for NED.)

It seems your friend has arrived to tell you the same thing.

(NED turns. The BEAR sees him and lopes past the others, standing when he comes to NED and holding out his arms. He cries with relief—as though he speaks NED's name. NED embraces him.)

Will you take him with you to your ditch, Master Lowenscroft? Or will you send him back to the pit? Not much difference, is there?

HARRY: There will be no ditch, Madam. And no return to the pit.

ELIZABETH: You redeem the name of *Harry*, Master Pearle. I only hope he heard you.

Scene Nine

(There is a commotion in the yard. Voices and dogs.)

CECIL: *(Off.)* Get down! Get *down!* Call them off, you idiot! *Call them off!!*

(Shouts and whistling quieten the dogs. NED takes the BEAR aside. The lights alter. CECIL enters from the courtyard.)

Madam ... Majesty.

ELIZABETH: *(Not turning.)* Is it done?

CECIL: Those dogs!

ELIZABETH: Forget the dogs. The *message.* Is it delivered?

CECIL: Yes.

(CECIL removes his hat and cloak and hands them to TARDY, who takes them to one of the skips.)

ELIZABETH: Did you ...? Was he present?

CECIL: Yes, Madam.

ELIZABETH: Did he speak?

CECIL: *(Going to the brazier.)* At length, Your Grace.

ELIZABETH: And?

CECIL: He requested of the Lord Lieutenant—that's Sir Walter Badger, Your Grace, a fine reliable fellow ...

ELIZABETH: I know his name! Come to the words.

CECIL: Madam, I am out of breath.

ELIZABETH: *His words.*

CECIL: His words. Yes. He requested that he see the communication of Your Majesty's decision with his own eyes.

ELIZABETH: And ...?

CECIL: And it was handed to him.

ELIZABETH: Pygmy!

CECIL: He read it—word for word—twice over.

ELIZABETH: Yes?

CECIL: And when, the second time, he came to Your Majesty's signature ...

ELIZABETH: What?

CECIL: He kissed it, Madam. Held it for an instant to his breast— and kissed it once again.

ELIZABETH: But what did he say? What did he say?

CECIL: He said, Your Grace, that he craved Your Majesty's forgiveness.

ELIZABETH: Forgiveness. But not my pardon?

CECIL: Madam, your letter expressly stated there would be no pardon.

(The bell tolls the hour of six. Silence.)

ELIZABETH: And ...?

CECIL: And ... he submitted to Your Majesty's will.

ELIZABETH: Without a word of protest?

CECIL: None.

ELIZABETH: Was he—is he … afraid?

CECIL: Yes.

ELIZABETH: Was it said? Did he say so—*I am afraid.*

CECIL: It was put to him by a priest that, being mortal, his Lordship might be fearful, and—"yes," he said. "Yes, I am. More than once, in battle," he said, "I have been seized by fears I had not imagined possible. But this is worse, because tomorrow is a certainty and if the strength of God is not with me in the morning, I will not know how to stand."

ELIZABETH: He said this?

CECIL: "I am young," he said … *(Relishing the words.)* "… and I have spent my youth in wantonness, lust, and filth. I have been puffed up with pride and vanity. My sins are more in number than the hairs on my head," he said. And at this point, Madam, he fell to his knees.

ELIZABETH: And … the Queen. Did he speak of the Queen?

CECIL: In this way only. Still on his knees, he said to me: "Here before you, I pray for the welfare of Her Majesty the Queen, whose death I protest I never meant. Nor any violence to her person." Then he said: "Say so, Robert. Tell her I said so." And I have done as I was charged.

ELIZABETH: Did he not mention his offence? Nothing of his treason?

CECIL: Nothing of his treason. Only his sins. And his fear.

> *(Silence.)*

ELIZABETH: I want to see him.

CECIL: Your Majesty knows that cannot happen.

ELIZABETH: I want to see him.

CECIL: It cannot be allowed. These events must not be reversed. England and Your Majesty would suffer if they were.

ELIZABETH: You think *this* is not suffering? I want to see him!!

CECIL: Madam, you may not. *(To WILL.) And she will not!*

> *(WILL shrugs. He wants her to go for Southampton's sake.)*

ELIZABETH: Someone … someone take me to him. Someone bring him to me. Someone—do something!!

HENSLOWE: Madam—Your Grace—I beg you not to go. For your own sake. The dead are dead.

ELIZABETH: But I must. I must go. I must.

CECIL: Madam—no.

ELIZABETH: Then, send out the horses. Send out the messengers ...

HENSLOWE: The horses will fall.

ELIZABETH: *One* could arrive.

CECIL: The roads are foul, Madam. Mud—snow—ice. There is no time to reach the destination you require of horses. It is impossible.

ELIZABETH: *No!!*

CECIL: Yes.

ELIZABETH: Oh, God. So ... here we are—in the moment. *(She sits.)* You, sir—Master Edmund ...

> *(JACK goes to her. She stares at him.)*

You were once, to me, so beautiful ... *(She touches his face.)* And once, you were all my life.

JACK: Madam, yet again you mistake me.

ELIZABETH: Hush. Be still. I know who you are—another Irish upstart—with opinions counter to my own. And yet, you embody his beauty—and for that reason, you are forgiven.

> *(JACK retreats.)*

Elizabeth Rex. (To WILL.) There's your title, sir. *Elizabeth Rex, the Queen.* Have me say that "all my life, for the sake of my kingdom, I have played the Prince." And have me say that, "for the sake of my kingdom, I willingly took up the sword of the Headsman and brought it down where I would rather kiss." And have me say ... Have me say ...

STANLEY: Madam ...

ELIZABETH: I cannot achieve this moment. How does one say *goodbye?*

NED: I can show you.

ELIZABETH: You would go to the Tower in my place?

NED: I would go in your person.

CECIL: Never. This must not happen.

WILL: It strikes me, Your Majesty, my Lord Cecil is too anxious to keep you from the Tower. He fears the woman in you might undo his present and his future powers.

CECIL: Prattle.

WILL: Is it?

CECIL: I will not argue this. She will not go. And none shall go in her place.

NED: Person. *(He smiles.)* There's a difference.

> *(The lights alter.*
>
> *There is music and the sound of water. A falcon cries overhead. Voices.)*
>
> *(Echo effect.)* Robin?
>
> *(JACK steps forward into a pool of light.)*

JACK: *(Echo effect.)* Madam?

> *(The echo effect fades over the next few speeches.)*

NED: No, not Madam. Not Majesty. Don't you remember?

JACK: What, Madam?

NED: My name. My *name.*

JACK: Elizabeth …

> *(Falcon cry.)*

NED: Not *Elizabeth. Bess.*

> *(NED moves into the light. They face each other.)*

You were my Robin—I was your Bess. I have come to die with you.

> *(JACK falls to his knees. NED caresses his head.)*

We will die together. Which is fitting. In killing you—I kill myself. How did we come to this moment?

JACK: Love.

NED: No. Ambition. You to be you—and me to be me.

> *(ELIZABETH moves into the light. JACK embraces NED's waist.)*

JACK: I love you.

NED: Yes. And I you. Nothing will remain of me when you are gone. I renege my right to the man who killed you. He is dead—and only I am left.

ELIZABETH: *(She reaches out.)* Robin?

> *(Falcon cry.*
>
> *The light fades on NED and JACK, and rises on WILL.)*

WILL: Would you go there? To be with him?

ELIZABETH: No. He is gone.

WILL: Madam, you, too, can conjure him.

ELIZABETH: I don't know how.

WILL: Yes, you do.

(Falcon cry.

ELIZABETH looks up, shading her eyes.)

You called him once your *hawk*. He sat on your arm.

ELIZABETH: Yes.

WILL: Call him.

ELIZABETH: Where is he?

(The light rises on NED. He has shed his white robe and wears tights and shirt.)

NED: Here, Bess. With you.

(ELIZABETH falls to her knees.)

Are you afraid?

ELIZABETH: Yes. Yes. More than once, I have been seized by fears I had not imagined possible—in the dark—in the night—but tomorrow is a certainty—and if your love is not with me in the morning, I will not know how to rise.

NED: You will rise. And I will rise with you. Stand.

ELIZABETH: I will not ask pardon. And there will be none. I have already said so. In this moment it is you who must die. But inside this moment, you will always be present. You were here—and you left your mark. Indelible. On me—and on the time.

NED: Am I to be proud of this?

ELIZABETH: No, Robin. You are to glory in it. *I* did not come here— I could not—but in my heart, I came.

(ELIZABETH leaves the light and retreats. NED is left alone in the pool of light.

Falcon cry.)

NED: *(Looking up.)* Hal …? Harry …? Hal …? How does one do this? I've done it a hundred times on stage. But you … you had to suffer it. And did. On that day, you rose from your bed thinking there was still *forever*. Yet in the afternoon—in the evening—in the twilight—you sank into the earth. Out of all sight forever. How does one do this? How? To be alive—no more. No more the smell of horses or the kiss of leather. No more connections, no more responses. *(He looks at WILL.)* No more wonder. No more words. *(He looks at HARRY.)* No more the warmth of breath—or the touch of fingertips on skin. Of all these joys—no more. All the way over. You're gone. You're safe. Safe. *(He goes to ELIZABETH.)* Madam, here is your man. If I can let him go—I can go myself.

(The bell begins to toll seven. Everyone is frozen and silent. There is distant cannon fire. The dogs begin to bark. The cannon in the yard is fired. There is a frenzy of barking.

ELIZABETH gives a cry.

Everyone remains still and silent.)

Scene Ten

(The lights alter.)

CECIL: Madam, the hour for matins has arrived.

ELIZABETH: Has it? So, you would go to pray?

CECIL: I pray every day, Majesty.

ELIZABETH: Do you? I would not have guessed it.

CECIL: Yes—I do. Every day.

ELIZABETH: Why? You need not fear, Robert. You will survive me. You are too clever not to.

(CECIL bows and exits. ELIZABETH addresses everyone.)

The curfew is lifted—I will leave you now. I thank you for your company. I played here as a child—and I have played this night— in this sweet, good place—my final days. *(To MATT.)* Sir, I am not blind. *(Taking STANLEY's hand.)* You, my dear one, all that I might have been, may you have all I might have had. I bless you.

(She kisses STANLEY's brow and joins her hand in MATT's. ELIZABETH turns to TARDY.)

You, Mistress, this *(A ring.)* ... is for you. And I pray, as it was for me, a token of some fidelity. I had it from my Lord Burleigh. Until his final breath, he was my protector. *(To WILL.)* For you, sir, my words. Use them as you will. I cannot offer you more. Though one thing else would be welcome. Your Lord in the Tower shall keep his head. But while I live, he will lose his freedom. *(To JACK.)* For you—a sample of your hatred.

(She goes to STANLEY and removes a locket in which there is a miniature portrait of herself.)

(To STANLEY.) In ridding you of this, I rid you of your vows.

STANLEY: But, Madam—that is your portrait. I ...

ELIZABETH: You will not miss it. You have me in your heart. *(She goes to JACK.)* This, sir, is all you need to avenge your loss of Ireland. An object on which you may relieve yourself as you will—to no avail. Ireland is mine. *(Then, to PERCY.)* Come with me. Here ...

PERCY: Madam.

ELIZABETH: "Oh, Fool—I shall go mad ..." *(She kisses him. Then she turns to NED.)* Master Lowenscroft—I would rather I had known you than anyone, but one, I ever met. I will not forget you. *(To HARRY.)* Nor you, sir. Nor the bear.

(She caresses the BEAR's face and gives him a honey cake. Then she removes her ropes of pearls and places them around the BEAR's neck.)

These, I trust, will keep you both from your ditch.

(She looks all around.)

Come, Countess—let us go together.

(LUDDY steps forward expectantly.)

LUDDY: "God save your Grace."

(ELIZABETH ignores him. LUDDY falls to his knees, devastated. ELIZABETH and HENSLOWE exit. The others follow— NED, HARRY, and the BEAR.)

WILL: *(Turning to the audience.)* And so, it was done. We had our man—we had our woman—and this way, they passed into time.

(CECIL returns.)

CECIL: Master Shakespeare—a word. This story must remain within these walls—for our mutual benefit in the time to come.

(He exits.

A passing bell is heard.

WILL blows out a lantern and takes another in hand. He pockets his notebook and removes the scholar's cap, kisses it, and places it on top of the severed head.)

WILL: Young Will Shakespeare died this day. Fifty-two years old. Died in his bed. A man of talent, who had an uneventful life. Or so it will be said.

(We hear the sound of water, birds, and insects.)

BOYS: *(Calling from the past.)* Will! Will! Over here—over here!

(WILL makes a slow exit into the yard.

The bell continues to toll.

The lights fade until only the sky is lit. Then, blackout.

The play ends.)